D0833188

DESIGNING HEALTH COMMUNICATION CAMPAIGNS:

WHAT WORKS?

DESIGNING HEALTH COMMUNICATION CAMPAIGNS: WHAT WORKS?

THOMAS E. BACKER
EVERETT M. ROGERS
PRADEEP SOPORY

SAGE Publications
International Educational and Professional Publisher
Newbury Park   London   New Delhi

Copyright © 1992 by Sage Publications, Inc.

All rights reserved. No part of this book may be reproduced or utilized in any form or by any means, electronic or mechanical, including photocopying, recording, or by any information storage and retrieval system, without permission in writing from the publisher.

For information address:

SAGE Publications, Inc.
2455 Teller Road
Newbury Park, California 91320

SAGE Publications Ltd.
6 Bonhill Street
London EC2A 4PU
United Kingdom

SAGE Publications India Pvt. Ltd.
M-32 Market
Greater Kailash I
New Delhi 110 048 India

Printed in the United States of America

Library of Congress Cataloging-in-Publication Data

Backer, Thomas E.
    Designing health communication campaigns: what works? / Thomas E.
Backer, Everett M. Rogers, Pradeep Sopory.
        p.   cm.
    Includes bibliographical references.
    ISBN 0-8039-4331-8.—ISBN 0-8039-4332-6 (pbk.)
    1. Mass media in health education.   2. Communication in medicine.
I. Rogers, Everett M.   II. Sopory, Pradeep.   III. Title.
RA440.55.B33   1992
362.1′014—dc20   92-6165
                                                                       CIP

92 93 94 95 10 9 8 7 6 5 4 3 2 1

Sage Production Editor: Chiara C. Huddleston

Contents

Introduction   ix

Part One: Overview   1

The Challenge of Health Behavior Change   2
One Solution: Health Communication Campaigns   3
Two Examples of Health Communication Campaigns   7
The Comparative Synthesis Study   14
Substance Abuse and High-Risk Youth   19
Setting the Agenda for the Issue of Drugs   21

Part Two: Generalizations About Health Communication Campaigns   29

Overview   29
Generalizations About Health Communication Campaigns   30
Discussion   32

Part Three: Interviews With Campaign Designers/Experts   35

Elaine Bratic Arkin
Georgetown University   36

Warren J. Ashley
Entertainment Industry Coalition on AIDS   40

Charles Atkin
Michigan State University   46

Thomas E. Backer
Human Interaction Research Institute   51

Edwin Chen
Los Angeles Times   57

Patrick C. Coleman
Johns Hopkins University   60

Larry Deutchman
Entertainment Industries Council   65

Brian Dyak
Entertainment Industries Council   71

Fern Field
Brookfield Productions   75

Juan M. Flavier
International Institute of Rural Reconstruction, Philippines   78

Brian Flay
University of Illinois   81

June Flora
Stanford University   84

Vicki Freimuth
University of Maryland   89

Kipling J. Gallion
The University of Texas at Austin   93

Robert W. Gillespie
Population Communications   99

Robert Hornik
University of Pennsylvania   102

Jose Ruben Jara
Institute for Communication Research   107

C. Anderson Johnson
University of Southern California   110

Marcy Kelly
Mediascope   114

Lawrence Kincaid
Johns Hopkins University   120

David McCallum
Center for Risk Communication   123

Jacqueline E. McDonald
Scott Newman Center   128

John V. Pavlik
Freedom Forum Media Studies Center   134

Mary Ann Pentz
University of Southern California   138

Ronald E. Rice
Rutgers University   145

Everett M. Rogers
University of Southern California   149

Charles Salmon
University of Wisconsin—Madison   153

Larry Stewart
Entertainment Industries Council   158

Lawrence Wallack
University of California at Berkeley   161

Part Four: Implications and Future Directions   167

Implications for Campaign Design   167
Implications for Future Research   172

References   177

About the Authors   181

Introduction

Much has been written in the last 10 years about health communication campaigns, especially those using mass media as a prime component. This is so for several reasons: First, empirical evidence has shown these campaigns to be effective in initiating or changing important behaviors related to health; second, the sheer number of campaigns has increased in the United States and abroad; third, aggressive efforts to promote health and prevent disease have risen higher on the American social agenda; and fourth, interest in studying campaigns has heightened, in part because of the first three factors. This interest has been generated in both the social sciences and mass communication fields, and increasingly has involved the work not only of university-based scholars, but also of professionals based in independent research settings, in health care institutions, in federal health agencies, and in community nonprofit organizations devoted to health and social issues.

Several good books are currently available about mass media health campaigns—Rice and Atkin's (1989) *Public Communication Campaigns*, Salmon's (1990) *Public Information Campaigns*, and Atkin and Wallack's (1990) *Mass Communication and Public Health*, for example. Each of these works presents studies and commentaries about health communication campaigns in a variety of topical areas.

These books and others use the terms *health communication, public communication,* and *public information campaigns* somewhat interchangeably. Most of the campaigns examined in these works are centrally organized around mass media (television, radio, print ads, and the like), although they also typically include community action and interpersonal approaches as well. In this book, we restrict our coverage to communication campaigns that feature a mass media component and that are intended to have an impact on health behavior.

As we contemplated writing this book, we began with a straightforward question: *Why another book about these campaigns?* This introduction analyzes what we believe to be this particular work's place on the bookshelf in terms of both the sources of its ideas and its overall aims.

This volume is the first product of a sequence of studies conducted by Thomas Backer and Everett Rogers, the first with Pradeep Sopory, on three aspects of mass media health campaigns that have previously received little attention in the burgeoning literature on this subject:

(1) *The development of generalizations* to answer the basic question, "What works?" through the comparative synthesis of campaign experiences in widely different topical areas. Until recently, the body of empirical evidence on successful health campaigns that include a mass media component was too limited and scattered to permit cross-comparison. Now there is much more evidence and experience to study, but most campaign scholars deal with one or a limited number of specific health topics in their studies. Further progress requires comparing campaigns on drug abuse with those on population control, AIDS, and so forth, to look for common principles and the most effective intervention strategies. Our first study undertook this comparative synthesis through an extensive review of the literature and interviews with prominent campaign designers. We deliberately used a *qualitative* rather than a quantitative approach, in order to identify broad generalizations about the basic question "What works?" with the hope that empirical investigation of some of these themes would follow. Moreover, many campaigns in recent years have begun with some reinventing of the wheel because their designers were not even aware of what had worked in other topical areas, so comparative synthesis is of *practical* and *economic* value as well.

(2) *Study of the characteristics, experiences, philosophies, and creative styles of campaign designers*, those who shape campaigns and direct their subsequent operation. Strong personalities and well-honed philosophies about health behavior change and about mass media, high levels of personal commitment, and often considerable personal charisma tend to characterize those who work in the mass media campaign field. These factors are likely to have a significant impact on both the nature of campaigns and their success.

(3) *Study of the characteristics of organizations involved in health communication campaigns*, and how these organizations work together to either facilitate or inhibit the success of mass media campaigns. The organizational and interorganizational dynamics of mass media health campaigns—which tend to be complex, highly interdependent enterprises—have a significant bearing on campaign outcome, but these factors are virtually virgin territory in research on campaigns.

This book addresses the first two factors, and a work in preparation addresses the third (Backer & Rogers, 1992). Research agendas about mass media health campaigns can be set for years to come with the issues raised under these three themes. However, we also see some very practical purposes being served by our work. First, *students* of campaigns may find it useful to have the present book on the shelf next to one or more texts about campaign design, to provide a richer interpretive context for learning about campaigns. Second, *designers* of campaigns may find inspiration for the structure of future campaigns here, and also questions they can pose to themselves about how their values and styles influence the campaigns they conduct. Increasingly, ways of thinking about scientific research suggest that the challenge is not to eliminate such "personal bias," which usually is not possible anyway, but rather to label it clearly, try to understand it, and actually *use* it in productive ways.

In Part I, we address in some detail a related phenomenon that we think helps to account for both the visibility and the success of many recent health communication campaigns—the rise of a health issue on the *public and media agenda*. To understand the larger social and environmental context in which a campaign operates, we must analyze where a particular campaign topic sits on the public and media agenda. Because the central focus of this book's *content* is on substance abuse, we have provided some specific background about how drug abuse became an item high on the public and media agenda in the United States.

When a health issue is high on the public and media agenda, "natural energy" is provided that can greatly help a campaign to be successful. While campaign designers may have little influence over the rise of an issue on the agenda, they certainly can benefit from understanding this element of *timing* and using good timing to their advantage. Knowing something about *why* an issue rises on the public and media agenda also can be invaluable to campaign design.

In Part IV, we also outline briefly another topic our research has shown is having increasing impact on campaign design: the use of *entertainment* media and techniques, as focused in the "entertainment-education" strategy. This approach provides unique energy sources for helping to overcome some of the barriers to campaign success that have been identified in much recent research.

Substance abuse—abuse of alcohol and street or prescription drugs—is a special emphasis of our analysis in this book. This is partly because campaigns on this subject are common today, and are the subject of much popular and scholarly attention, and partly because the funding support for the present work was provided by the Office for Substance Abuse Prevention (OSAP). Some special findings related to *substance abuse prevention with high-risk youth* are presented throughout this book, and are described in greater detail in the final report of our first OSAP study (Backer, Rogers, & Sopory, 1990), and in portions of our annotated bibliography (Backer, Rogers, & Sopory, 1991).

We see these briefly presented findings on substance abuse prevention and high-risk youth as having value beyond their interest to those conducting campaigns in this particular subject area. A main tenet of this book is that most of the factors associated with effective mass media campaigns are not, in fact, highly specific to those campaigns' topics. And, as will also be made clear by the 29 interviews that form the heart of this book, campaign designers have many styles and precepts in common, even though they may work in very different subject areas. However, there are some elements of campaign design that *are* specific to a particular subject area. The brief summary given here about substance abuse prevention campaigns can help to reinforce this point. Readers interested in other campaign topics are encouraged to think creatively about how the factors identified here for substance abuse prevention and high-risk youth might need to be altered to reflect the realities in their own areas of interest.

We stress substance abuse prevention campaigns in the present volume for another reason: The rise of drug abuse on the social and media agenda has increased both the *demand* and the *opportunity* for such campaigns. For example, DARE (Drug Abuse Resistance Education) campaigns began only in 1983 in Los Angeles, but reached 4.5 million schoolchildren in 1989-1990 (see Backer & Rogers, in press, for a detailed analysis of the DARE program). DARE, which has included a media component, centers on an interpersonal training strategy in which a uniformed police officer teaches a 19-hour curriculum about drug abuse to fifth and sixth graders. Why did DARE diffuse so widely in the United States and in so few years? One reason is that the U.S. population perceives the drug problem as very serious, as analyzed later in this book. In such a climate of urgency, there is a shared expectation between community and government that "we have to do something," and the opportunity increases for such efforts to start, along with public demand that these programs be encouraged and supported.

We have chosen two examples of "mass media health campaigns" to provide a brief overview for those who may not already be familiar with the content or context of these campaigns. Both campaigns happen to concern the physical health problem of heart disease. Both also include mass media components in the context of a larger community-based effort. The Stanford Heart Disease Prevention Program, launched in 1971 in three (later in five) California communities, and the North Karelia Project, begun at the same time, in the province of Finland with the highest rates of cardiovascular disease in the world, are our two widely known examples.

We chose these two examples in large part because they are extremely well documented and they have been successful, and because a host of other campaigns to promote healthy life-styles have been designed using the approaches developed first by these two projects. So many campaigns have emerged from these two, in fact, that some of the "great-grandchildren" and "great-great-grandchildren" of the Stanford and North Karelia campaigns do not even recognize their ancestry! One of the authors once constructed a "family tree" for these health communication campaigns, but the chart became so busy after two generations that it became difficult to understand. The Stanford and North Karelia efforts and their empirical evaluations showed that campaigns could successfully fulfill their goals, a perception that in part explains why so many health communication campaigns have been conducted since the 1970s.

Many of the campaigns reviewed here are intended to bring about some type of *preventive health behavior.* Examples include smoking cessation, exercise, and dietary changes to reduce the risk of heart disease or cancer; drug abuse prevention; the designated driver concept to reduce drunk driving; sexual abstinence and contraception to reduce the likelihood of unwanted pregnancy; and safe sex to reduce the chance of HIV infection leading to AIDS. Preventive behavior is a particularly difficult goal to achieve through mass media campaigns. An individual must change behavior *now* by taking a preventive action (which is often unpleasant in nature) in order to lower the probability of some unwanted *future* event that may not happen anyway.

For example, research on the effects of an auto seat belt campaign in Indiana found that while two-thirds of all Indiana adults were reached by the campaign's messages, no increase in seat belt use resulted (Gantz, Fitzmaurice, & Yoo, 1990). Why not? First, even though every vehicle in Indiana is equipped with seat belts, most people regard them as unpleasant to use: They soil or wrinkle clothes and they are constraining, uncomfortable, or even painful to wear. Further, most respondents in the Indiana study perceived that the likelihood of their having vehicle accidents was very low, so they rationalized seat belt use as unnecessary. Some Indiana adults even believed that seat belt use at the time of an accident would lower their chances of survival. So communication campaigns of a preventive nature, as many health campaigns are, face special difficulties in achieving behavior change, at least compared with "nonpreventive campaigns," such as political campaigns or activities to diffuse and promote the use of a new product or service.

Nevertheless, a number of more recent preventive campaigns, especially on health topic areas, have been relatively successful. Compared with the pre-1971 era of mass media health campaign experiences, when most evaluations showed that these campaigns failed, more recent campaigns, and especially *preventive* health campaigns, have had greater chances of success for the following reasons:

(1) They have been based on vigorous, empirically validated *social science theories*, such as social learning theory, social marketing, the health belief model, and the diffusion of innovations.

(2) They have utilized *formative evaluation research* in order to improve the effectiveness of the communication campaign before it was launched or while it was under way.

(3) In comparison with earlier campaigns, they have had *more reasonable objectives* (e.g., a goal of achieving a 3% reduction in the risk of heart disease in a four-year campaign) that are more likely to be reached.

Modern-day campaigns can still fail, as the Indiana auto seat belt campaign illustrates, but the likelihood of success overall is greater. Such optimism is probably one reason for the large number of mass media health campaigns that are currently being carried out.

We would like to convey our thanks to Robert Denniston, our project officer at the Office for Substance Abuse Prevention (which funded the research on which this book is based), for his participation in shaping our work. We also thank the campaign experts who shared with us the lessons they had learned about health communication campaigns. Gratitude is also due to the staff of the Human Interaction Research Institute, for their assistance with our research and with preparation of this book. Finally, we acknowledge the USC Annenberg School for Communication and its dean, Dr. Peter Clarke, for many inputs to the present endeavor.

So here is a book about mass media campaigns for health, based on theoretical perspectives and written by social scientists, that is intended to be practically useful to campaign designers and to students of health communication campaigns. We hope that our readers find its lessons learned to be interesting and of practical value in guiding future campaigns and their study.

THOMAS E. BACKER
LOS ANGELES, CALIFORNIA

EVERETT M. ROGERS
LOS ANGELES, CALIFORNIA

PRADEEP SOPORY
MADISON, WISCONSIN

PART ONE

Overview

The great American actress Helen Hayes once said, "It's what you learn after you know it all that really counts." Designers of health communication campaigns often have considerable expertise about the particular areas of health behavior that they are attempting to change, and about specific media techniques such as television or radio public service announcements (PSAs). But campaign designers and researchers seldom examine what works and what does not in campaigns on health topics *other* than their primary interests, and they often have only incomplete understanding of how the industries that produce and distribute media products (film, television, and so on) operate. The impacts of their campaigns inevitably suffer as a result, no matter how well designed they otherwise may be.

Here we provide a *comparative synthesis* of what works and what does not in health communication campaigns across a large number of topical areas that have a mass media component. Because our research for this book was sponsored by the Office for Substance Abuse Prevention (OSAP), first priority was given to the exploration of alcohol and other drug abuse prevention campaigns for high-risk youth. However, we also review campaigns on such other topics as AIDS, smoking, teenage pregnancy, heart disease, Alzheimer's disease, and vehicle seat belt use.

A comparative synthesis over such a wide range of health topics and a broad variety of campaign strategies presents many challenges. It is our hope that the synthesis found herein can lead to the rethinking of conventional wisdom, to the development of new research hypotheses, and to the formulation of innovative strategies for campaign design.

The second principal goal of this book, and particularly of the 29 interviews that are its main content, is to explore the impact on campaign design and effectiveness of the personal characteristics, beliefs, and experiences of *campaign designers.* To our knowledge, this has not been done before in a systematic way. This book therefore represents the first effort to look at how these personal aspects of the people who design campaigns affect the campaigns themselves. Even though the content of the interviews (see below) is clearly focused on the nature of campaigns themselves, the personal element comes through strongly in each interview. Such a perspective can help us to understand current and past campaigns better, and to design future campaigns more effectively.

This book does *not* provide a thorough explanation or critical review of health communication campaign theory, history, or components. For this the reader is referred to several recent analyses, such as Salmon (1990), Rice and Atkin (1989), and Atkin and Wallack (1990). There is an extensive literature on this subject, which we review in the study reported here, and which is more fully detailed in a separate annotated bibliography (Backer et al., 1991) described later in this section. This literature addresses in much more detail the generalizations derived from our study.

The Challenge of Health Behavior Change

Advances in health care have made extraordinary differences in the life expectancy and level of vitality of the average American. Despite such "medical miracles," however, the U.S. surgeon general says that one-half of all premature deaths—that is, deaths occurring before the age of normal life expectancy—are preventable. Most of these preventable deaths have to do with culturally sustained behavior and life-style factors (U.S. Department of Health, Education and Welfare, 1979). As discussed in the introduction to this volume, preventive behavior change is extremely difficult to achieve.

For instance, in 1985, the U.S. Department of Health and Human Services estimated that 771,000 people died of heart disease, 462,000 of cancer, and 46,000 in auto accidents. Many of these deaths can be directly attributed to life-style and behavior factors, such as cigarette smoking.

More than 200,000 cases of AIDS were diagnosed in the United States by early 1991, and more than half of these persons had already died (as estimated by the Centers for Disease Control). The actual number of deaths from AIDS is probably much higher, given the under-reporting of AIDS deaths, especially in the early 1980s. Use of safer sex practices or avoiding needle sharing could have prevented most of these deaths from AIDS.

Thousands of people die each year from drug overdoses, or from the effects of drug-related violence and accidents, or from health complications of drug abuse. Many more die from the effects of alcohol abuse. We do not know exactly how many.

Society as a whole must pay the price for these deaths and illnesses, in terms of rising health care costs. More than 11% of the gross national product in the United States is devoted to health care. Despite vigorous efforts by government and the private sector, health care cost containment remains elusive.

The rise of health and fitness trends in all sectors of U.S. society is a hopeful sign, as a "revolution" in healthy life-styles has occurred in recent decades. A growing awareness of how much we are paying for health services may eventually reduce the burden of rising costs. But too many people still do not know all they need to know about reducing personal risks of compromised health, injury, and death—and far too many people do not act on what they know. There is a great need both for transmission of accurate health-related information and for active promotion of health behavior change in the United States.

One Solution: Health Communication Campaigns

While no societal problem of this magnitude has a single solution, health communication campaigns can help. Television, radio, film, and print media are increasingly being used in creative ways to present health information and to stimulate awareness, attitude change, and behavior change. Health communication campaigns typically have inter-personal (training, counseling) and community (neighborhood group, advocacy) components as well, and in the more sophisticated campaigns these various elements are carefully interwoven through an overall strategic design.

A campaign can be defined as having four essential ingredients (Rogers & Storey, 1987):

(1) A campaign is purposive, and seeks to influence individuals.
(2) A campaign is aimed at a large audience.
(3) A campaign has a more or less specifically defined time limit.
(4) A campaign involves an organized set of communication activities.

Most large-scale campaigns today depend upon broadcast television as their single most important communication channel, although newspapers, magazines, radio, cable television, videocassettes, and other media are also employed. Most communication campaigns are multimedia, on the assumptions that (a) each medium may get through to a somewhat unique subaudience and (b) multiple exposure to campaign messages will have greater effects. Some campaigns, such as Nancy Reagan's Just Say No efforts to prevent drug abuse by children, have reached very high levels of public visibility nationally, while others, such as the Stanford Heart Disease Prevention Program, have been much lower in public profile (although not in Northern California, where the program was implemented).

Increasing numbers of campaigns have been evaluated systematically, but many campaigns have not. Many campaigns have been described and analyzed in publicly available literature, but many campaigns (especially the failures) have not. So extracting what works and what does not from these various campaigns is a challenge.

While, as stated, this book is not intended to serve as a review of the theory and operation of health communication campaigns, we do need to begin our discussion of the study we conducted by presenting a few basic assumptions by which our study's analysis has been guided. Specifically, we view campaigns as having seven potential levels of effect on their audiences, each of which requires a certain evaluative strategy for measurement of effect. Table 1 presents these seven levels and an example of how each might be measured for a campaign. This paradigm is critical because it acknowledges that health communication campaigns may have different kinds of impacts, and different measures are needed to gauge these impacts.

TABLE 1 Hierarchy of Effects of a Communication Campaign and Sample Measures of Effects

Level of Effect	*Sample Measures of Effects*
(1) Audience *exposure* to message(s)	TV ratings
(2) Audience *awareness* of message(s)	audience survey
(3) Audience's being *informed* by message	audience survey
(4) Audience's being *persuaded* by message	audience survey
(5) Audience expression of *intent* to change behavior	audience survey
(6) Actual *change* in audience's behavior	point-of-referral monitoring for health source
(7) *Maintenance* of audience behavior change	point-of-referral monitoring for health source

Second, we regard most campaigns as including an effort to persuade individuals to adopt a specific *innovation*—for instance, the use of condoms or the selection of designated drivers. In general terms, an innovation is an idea perceived as new by an individual or by some other adopting unit, such as a community or an organization (Rogers, 1983). The idea may not be new in an absolute sense, but if it is perceived as new by the individual or organization, it necessarily entails risks and uncertainties that would not otherwise be present: Innovation adoption requires the individual or organization to change—and change is hard, often producing fears, resistance, and other potentially inhibiting reactions (Backer, 1991).

There are two types of innovations of specific concern to health communication campaigns: *incremental* and *preventive*. An example of an incremental innovation is an Iowa farmer planting hybrid seed corn so as to obtain a 20% increase in crop yield, or a Finnish Laplander purchasing a snowmobile for improved transportation. Notice that the individual decides to adopt the new idea now, at t_1, in order to gain an increment in a desired outcome at t_2, in the near-term future.

Preventive innovations are more difficult to diffuse rapidly. An individual must take an action (that is, adopt a life-style change) now, at t_1, in order to lower the probability of occurrence of an expected unwanted future event (such as heart disease, cancer, AIDS, or unwanted pregnancy) at t_2 (see Figure 1). The sought-after reward is distant in time, and may not happen even if the preventive action is taken. Under these conditions, it is understandable why individuals do not adopt preventive innovations easily or rapidly.

1. Incremental Innovation:

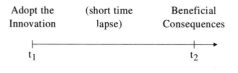

2. Preventive Innovation:

Figure 1. Preventive Innovations Are More Difficult to Diffuse Than Are Incremental Innovations.

Frequently, mass media campaigns concerning health issues involve communicating the findings from biomedical research almost as soon as they are generated. Today many of these findings are about *risk behaviors*. In areas ranging from AIDS to smoking to overweight, Americans are bombarded with information through the mass media about what behaviors are risky. To a lesser extent, they are also exposed to information regarding what behavioral scientists are learning about ways in which behavior can be changed—what strategies for individual behavior change work best, and how systems ranging from families to whole communities can help support the change process.

Because of the mass media's endless appetite for new subjects to report, and because of the increasing public interest in health and fitness topics, the media are not just a passive vehicle for health promotion. Health reporters are commonplace in newspapers, radio, and television, as are "disease of the week" television movies and documentaries that concentrate on characters with severe or life-threatening illnesses such as cancer or AIDS. Portrayals of various health issues in entertainment television programming are numerous, although research indicates that these images often are in serious conflict with what health professionals would agree are appropriate guidelines to good health (Signorielli, 1988). Health matters are also presented in news, information, and entertainment programming because of their commercial viability, as will be discussed further below. The mass media increasingly take an active role in disseminating information about risk behaviors in various areas of health and illness. Some media professionals and institutions feel that they have a social responsibility to do so.

A few evaluations of campaigns have been conducted with a high degree of rigor. Examples include smoking-cessation programs (see Flay, 1986) and heart disease prevention (see Maccoby & Solomon, 1981). Certain principles for success have emerged from these studies, as well as certain strategies that clearly do not work. In other campaigns, even without rigorous evaluation, guidelines and examples of success or failure are available that may have potential for wider utilization (at least when translated to a conceptual level), as in the generalizations presented later.

As DeJong and Winston (1989) observe in their analytic review of mass media campaigns, current research and professional attitudes about the role that mass media campaigns can play in changing health behavior fall somewhere between the excessively optimistic expectations of recent decades and the more recent realism based on evaluations of health campaigns that failed to take account of some important contextual factors. Gradual, long-term changes toward healthier lifestyles are occurring. The decreasing percentage of American adults who smoke is an example. Mass media campaigns can play a role in changing health behavior, but the changes are evolutionary, and are affected by many nonmedia factors. The Stanford Heart Disease Prevention Program and a smoking-cessation campaign in Australia are cited by DeJong and Winston as examples of long-term programs with mass media components that seem to have had powerful effects.

Two Examples of Health Communication Campaigns

Following are descriptions of two of the most successful and best-documented health behavior change campaigns that included significant mass media components: the North Karelia Project in Finland, and the Stanford Heart Disease Prevention Program in California. These are provided to give an overview of campaign designs, operations, and evaluations.

NORTH KARELIA PROJECT

In 1972, a preventive health campaign was begun in North Karelia, a province in Finland, in order to help the entire community reduce its risk factors associated with cardiovascular disease (Puska et al., 1979, 1981, 1985, 1986). The program was designed in response to a 1971 petition signed by the people of North Karelia Province, after statistics showed that the province had the highest levels of cardiovascular disease in Finland, and Finland then had the highest rate of any nation in the world. The petition asked for a government-supported public health program, which was assisted by international experts from the World Health Organization and by local leaders who planned a course of action.

The North Karelia Project was designed and evaluated by Dr. Pekka Puska and his colleagues at the National Public Health Institute in Helsinki, with much of the conduct of the campaign activities carried out by local leaders and through community organizations. The National Public Health Institute is perceived as a relatively prestigious, credible sponsor of the North Karelia Project by the people in North Karelia Province.

The project implemented a heart disease risk-reduction program on a communitywide scale. Experts felt that the program should be integrated into the social and health service structure of the community, because "behavior is embedded in a complex way in the social and physical environment" (Puska et al., 1986, p. 13). Because the problem of heart disease in North Karelia and in Finland in general was a "mass epidemic," the best solution was to implement a "mass intervention" (p. 9). North Karelia served as a pilot study for the entire country, to test the feasibility of involving the local community in such a preventive health program. Fortunately, medical and public health authorities felt they were in a good position to reduce the risk factors in the population that were due to smoking, elevated cholesterol, and high blood pressure. An accumulated tradition of biomedical research findings had established the likelihood that a decrease in these risk factors would lead to decreased cardiovascular disease rates.

The mass media components of this campaign included a series of seven television broadcasts to the people of North Karelia Province, dealing with smoking cessation as a major aspect of heart disease prevention. Posters and print advertisements promoting heart-healthy behaviors also were used as part of the campaign.

How did Finland come to have such relatively high rates of cardiovascular disease in 1971? In part, this problem came about as the result of rising incomes in the first several decades following World War II, which led to higher consumption of fats (through increasing consumption of butter, red meat, and other high-cholesterol foods). Many Finnish people continued to eat a traditional diet that had been appropriate when they were engaged in hard physical work, such as farming and lumbering, often in subzero conditions. But as the majority of Finns became information workers and settled into more sedentary life-styles, their diets had to change if they were to maintain good health.

Looked at this way, the problem of high rates of cardiovascular disease in Finland in 1971 was due to a "lagged feedback" regarding significant changes in Finnish society. Occupational and other social changes occurred in Finland, but nutrition, exercise, and other life-style changes lagged behind. One function of the North Karelia Project was to catch up this cybernetic lag, by readjusting life-styles to the changed occupational situation of contemporary Finnish society.

The rate of adoption of an innovation typically approximates an S-shaped curve over time. At first, the number of adopters of the new idea are relatively few per unit of time. Then, when about 15% or 20-25% of the members of a system adopt, the rate of adoption "takes off" and the number of adopters per unit of time begins to increase rapidly (see Figure 2). The priority strategy in diffusing an innovation among the members of a system consists of reaching this *critical mass.* Thereafter, the innovation will continue to diffuse in a self-sustaining process. We define the critical mass as the point in time at which enough individuals have adopted an innovation so that the perceived cost-benefit of adoption becomes positive for most individuals, and so that the rate of adoption of an innovation becomes self-sustaining. At that point, the health professional can step out of the picture, and the innovation will continue to diffuse under its own momentum.

The notion of a critical mass implies that relatively large campaign inputs are required early in the diffusion process of an innovation, but that after a certain number of individuals have adopted, the innovation will diffuse under its own power. The critical mass occurs because satisfied adopters of the idea are telling peers about their favorable experiences with the innovation. This is the state of affairs that was actively promoted by the designers of the North Karelia campaign.

The critical mass notion also implies that the diffusion of an innovation starts out relatively slowly. The effects of health promotion campaigns are cumulative, like a stalactite dripping, dripping, dripping. Slowly, the audience effects are built up. This phenomenon is illustrated

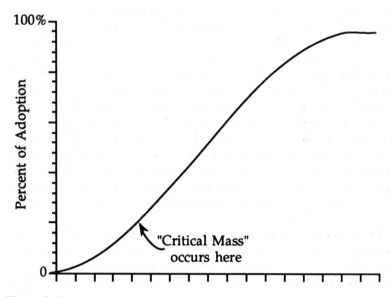

Figure 2. The Rate of Adoption of an Innovation

clearly by the North Karelia Project, which began 20 years ago. After
two decades of long-term commitment and continued funding, certain
means of reducing the risk of cardiovascular disease are now being
mounted that could not have been tried in a shorter project of only 5-10
years. For example, the massive shift from dairy farming to raising
berries in North Karelia is a basic economic change that has direct
health benefits. The professional staff of the North Karelia Project are
collaborating with supermarkets, bread companies, and other businesses to decrease the fat, sugar, and salt content of prepared foods, to
replace animal fat (for instance, butter) with rapeseed oil and marga-
rine, and to change consumer behavior from the use of whole milk to
nonfat milk. These important dietary changes could not have occurred
in North Karelia until a trust relationship between health professionals
and the public was created. That takes time.

The North Karelia Project recently sought to energize community
support for reducing heart disease risk by sponsoring a village-to-
village cholesterol-reduction competition. A number of villages entered
this competition by having at least 80% of their residents measured for
their blood cholesterol levels before and after the six-month competition.

The winning village achieved a 10% reduction in average cholesterol levels, and received the prize of a trip for two to Hawaii.

The North Karelia Project began to utilize opinion leaders in 1975, by recruiting them for participation in a two-day training seminar. About 800 opinion leaders were trained in healthy life-styles and encouraged to pass along this information to others. A 1982 survey, seven years after the initial training workshop in North Karelia, showed that half of the 800 opinion leaders were still active. The opinion leaders reported urging their friends and neighbors to stop smoking, to eat more vegetables, and to organize groups to watch the television quit-smoking programs that are a critical media component of the project. The use of opinion leaders in North Karelia was one strategy to help the healthy life-style promotion campaign reach a point of critical mass on the S-curve of diffusion.

The revolution in healthy life-styles that has been, and is, taking place in North Karelia represents a larger revolution in the nature of health education. Twenty years ago, health education meant one-to-one contact between a public health professional and a client. Today, health education means using a wide variety of communication channels, social marketing, social learning theory, and the like. One-to-one interpersonal communication may still be used, however, especially with opinion leaders, as it has been in North Karelia.

The major reductions in cardiovascular disease risk achieved by the North Karelia Project, the Stanford Heart Disease Prevention Program (discussed next), and their various "offspring" did not come about as the direct result of biomedical research breakthroughs. Instead, these life-saving advances occurred as the result of health education, but a new type of health education based on behavioral science research findings and theories. This accomplishment bodes well for several important public health challenges of today, such as the AIDS health crisis, which was ignored for too long in many countries (Rogers, Dearing, & Chang, 1991). Now we are seeking to gain control over this runaway epidemic, without a medical solution in hand or in sight. Clearly, communication campaigns for healthy life-styles, while they have achieved some sparkling successes, have a long way to go.

Social learning theory (discussed further in Part II) was utilized extensively in the design of messages for the North Karelia Project. For example, the 1978 Finnish television smoking-cessation campaign featured an in-studio group of 10 individuals who were carefully selected to represent each of the intended audience segments in the Finnish population that were targeted in the campaign, including, for instance, middle-aged men, young women, and teenaged males. Each of the 10 individuals was tracked during the seven television broadcasts, with each asked to tell about his or her resistances, difficulties, and achievements in learning to stop smoking. By the end of the seven-part television series, 8 of the 10 members of the in-studio smoking-cessation class had succeeded in quitting, and so had an estimated 10,000 other Finns, nationwide, at a total cost to the North Karelia Project of only $8,000 (the Finnish television network contributed the cost of broadcasting the programs).

The quit-smoking broadcasts had a greater effect in North Karelia Province (approximately double) than in the rest of Finland. Empirical study showed that the smoking-cessation campaign had greater effects in North Karelia because opinion leaders organized local television viewing groups there. Thus the effects of a campaign may rest in part on the degree to which community follow-through is carefully tied to a media effort.

Social learning theory also has been used by the North Karelia Project in developing a relationship with the local soccer team. The players wear the two-red-hearts logo of the North Karelia Project, and appear in posters and print advertisements promoting heart-healthy behaviors. The soccer players thus serve as positive role models for healthy life-styles.

STANFORD HEART DISEASE PREVENTION PROGRAM

About the same time (in 1971) that the North Karelia Project was getting under way, but unconnected with the Finnish project, a cardiologist (Dr. John Farquhar) and a communication scholar (Dr. Nathan Maccoby) at Stanford University designed the Stanford Heart Disease Prevention Program, which was funded by the National Institutes of Health. The program's first phase was carried out in three California communities. A second phase beginning in 1978 involved five California communities.

The Stanford Program consisted of a series of health communication activities aimed at smoking cessation, weight reduction, exercise, and stress reduction, all in order to reduce risk factors associated with heart disease. Both mass media communication approaches and interpersonal communication methods, such as small group training classes (for example, aerobic exercise classes and smoking-cessation classes) and networking of opinion leaders to their followers, were utilized in the Stanford Program.

The mass media components of the Stanford Program included television and radio, newspapers, and other mass-distributed print media. Education activities were also a part of the program, combining both face-to-face and media-based education in classes, contests, and correspondence courses. Special activities were developed for Spanish-language radio, newspapers, and mass-distributed print materials.

A continuous monitoring and evaluation process was carried out to measure the effects of the Stanford Program (Farquhar, Maccoby, Wood, & Alexander, 1977; Maccoby, Farquhar, & Solomon, 1984). Useful lessons about healthy life-style changes were learned from the program, even though the effects of each different subcampaign activity (for example, smoking cessation or dietary changes) could not be evaluated separately from the others, due to the bundled, integrated nature of the various campaign interventions.

In fact, this integrated design has been at the center of many of the program's greatest successes. For instance, the Stanford Program distributed small red heart-shaped magnets to hold "tip-sheets" on refrigerator doors. These magnets increased the visibility of heart disease prevention activities for both those who had healthy life-styles and those who visited the kitchens of the homes of the target audience in Northern California. The tip-sheets were an adaptation of the commercial marketing idea of point-of-sale display advertising, and contained program educational material. Moreover, the red heart logo was accompanied by a sound symbol in all radio and television spots used in the program. Such visual and auditory symbols tie all of the elements of a campaign together, providing easy identification for audience members and helping maximize the effects of the whole package of healthy life-style changes.

*   *   *

Over the past 20 years, the Finnish campaign designers and their Stanford counterparts have stayed in close contact about their mutual experiences with these two health communication campaigns. A great deal of useful exchange about preventive health strategies has occurred. A wide variety of campaigns concerning heart disease prevention, drug abuse prevention, smoking prevention, and the like are among the "children," "grandchildren," and "great-grandchildren" of the Stanford and North Karelia projects. In fact, as mentioned earlier, some of the offspring today do not recognize their ancestry. This extended family of life-style-oriented health communication campaigns today adds up to an important accumulation of worldwide experience.

The Comparative Synthesis Study

The inspiration for the research on which this book is based came when two of the authors (Backer and Rogers) participated with Robert Denniston of the Office for Substance Abuse Prevention in a conference on mass media and health (cosponsored by OSAP) at the Annenberg Center for Health Sciences in Rancho Mirage, California (Atkin & Arkin, 1988). At this 1988 conference, we observed that while many campaign strategies were discussed—and many of them seemed to have significant potential for wider use—little effort was being made to draw comparisons or to generalize. Thinking about the conceptual bridges that could be built across the campaigns led to our proposing a comparative synthesis of accumulated experiences with mass media health campaigns in a wide range of topical areas.

OSAP had already conducted a conference on effective media campaigns in June 1988, which brought together nine federal and private agencies to describe their media campaigns to prevent alcohol and other drug abuse problems. Although confined to this one topical area, the comparative approach used in this OSAP conference is similar to the design utilized in our subsequent research.

We combined a literature review and expert interviews because we felt this combination would provide the most adequate basis for beginning to cross-connect the available knowledge base about health campaigns. Both published and unpublished literature was included from a variety of sources, as described below. A wide range of expert interviews was included in our research. The Rancho Mirage conference made it clear that combining the lessons learned by scholars, media professionals, and campaign designers could be of much value in developing some generalizations that would hold up across campaign topical areas.

In addition, the supplemental generalizations about community-based substance abuse campaigns for high-risk youth contained in this book constitute one use of the rich and varied knowledge base about media campaigns that has been generated here. Much further analysis is possible; for example, we later present a suggestive scenario regarding campaigns for reducing stigma about mental illness as one way of utilizing some of what this study has produced.

The main steps involved in conducting the comparative synthesis study were as follows:

(1) *Development of an Analytic Framework.* We extended Rogers and Storey's (1987) definition of health communication campaigns with media components by creating an analytic framework (see Table 2) for investigating campaigns on various topics. The framework includes the types of *media components* (the delivery systems or communication channels for the campaign content), the types of *collaboration* (among both individuals and organizations), the *context* or environment in which the campaign is intended to have impact, the *structure* or procedural steps into which campaigns are organized, the *principles for what works* in a campaign, and the desired levels of *effects* of a campaign on its target audience. Each of these principles for "what works" in this preliminary framework appears in the list of 27 generalizations presented in Part II.

(2) *Comprehensive Literature Review.* We began by identifying a number of campaigns in various health behavior subject areas. Published and unpublished literature on the goals, designs, activities, and outcomes of campaigns were then identified for review. We placed particular emphasis on evaluative literature that extracted generalizations about campaign effectiveness from the standpoint of mass media professionals, health professionals, and outside third-party sponsors and consumers.

We used the following sources in our literature review:

- principal university libraries at the University of California at Los Angeles and the University of Southern California
- the extensive personal document collections of Rogers and Backer
- syllabi for relevant courses that Backer and Rogers teach at their universities (UCLA and USC, respectively)
- computer searches of the literature using standard search strategies
- inquiries to colleagues for unpublished or fugitive literature about health communication campaigns and their media components

TABLE 2   Campaign Analytic Framework

Media components
 (1) PSAs—radio and television
 (2) news programs—radio and television
 (3) information programs—radio and television (talk shows, interview shows,
     documentaries)
 (4) entertainment television programs—radio, soap operas, TV movies
 (5) celebrity personal appearances
 (6) fund-raising events
 (7) print media—newspaper, magazines, booklets
 (8) posters
 (9) feature films
(10) radio—discussion, interviews
(11) educational films/video
(12) special events—contests, awards

Structure of campaigns
 (1) setting objectives
 (2) evaluation research
 (3) collaborating individuals/groups
 (4) design
 (5) production
 (6) ongoing operation
 (7) formative evaluation
 (8) redevelopment
 (9) outcome evaluation

Effects
 (1) awareness
 (2) factual information
 (3) attitude
 (4) intention
 (5) behavior
 (6) continued use
 (7) maintenance

Collaborators
 (1) mass media
 (2) government
 (3) preventive health care professionals
 (4) community/advocacy leaders
 (5) media experts and expert organizations
 (6) media trade/professional organizations

Context
 (1) health care system
 (2) schools
 (3) family

TABLE 2 Continued
___

(4) workplace
(5) government
(6) community

Principles for what works
(1) Use multiple media.
(2) Combine media and interpersonal strategies.
(3) Segment audience.
(4) Use celebrities to get attention; entertainment programs to sustain attention.
(5) Provide simple, clear messages.
(6) Emphasize positive behavior more than negative consequences.
(7) Emphasize current rewards, not distant negative consequences.
(8) Involve key power figures and organizations.
(9) Take advantage of timing.
(10) Use formative evaluation.
___

We then reviewed the resulting literature base extensively. A preliminary synthesis culminated in our preparation of an annotated bibliography, with one- or two-paragraph annotations summarizing the intents, methods, and results of the various items included in the literature review. We also prepared an index to facilitate access to the annotations. (Copies of the annotated bibliography are available from the Human Interaction Research Institute, 1849 Sawtelle Blvd., Suite 102, Los Angeles, CA 90025; telephone [310] 479-3028.)

(3) *Campaign Designer Interviews.* Previous experiences of both Backer and Rogers with mass media health campaigns helped identify a number of potential expert interviewees, both in the United States and internationally, who are active in developing, conducting, or studying health campaigns. We felt that interviewees from other countries were of special importance because the relationships among the mass media, the public, and health behaviors vary somewhat in different countries.

We drew up a tentative list of more than 50 interviewees. The nominee list was neither comprehensive nor entirely representative, but it included a broad range of persons studying or working on mass media health behavior campaigns.

In the study that resulted, 29 interviews were conducted. Backer and Rogers were both interviewed themselves, both to pilot test the interview process and because both have significant practical campaign experience.

Interviews were targeted to answer the following questions:

(1) In what campaigns have you been involved (including campaigns targeted to substance abuse and high-risk youth), and what role did you play?

(2) What are the most common reasons mass media campaigns do not achieve their hoped-for results, and what are the most common reasons some campaigns are relatively successful?

(3) How could present health communication campaign models be improved to make them useful for planning, implementing, and evaluating mass media campaigns?

(4) What roles can formative or summative evaluation play in the relative success of a health communication campaign?

(5) What are the unique characteristics and special difficulties of preventive health communication campaigns, especially those aimed at high-risk youth?

(6) How do factors such as age groupings, fear appeals, audience segmentation, and use of opinion leaders contribute to the design of mass media campaigns targeted to high-risk youth?

(7) What is the most successful mass media campaign to change health behavior you have known, and why do you think it worked?

(8) What role should federal, state, or local governments play in media campaigns?

(9) What organizations and organizational factors contribute to the success or failure of media campaigns?

(10) What methods would you suggest for financing media campaigns for health?

Each interviewee was presented with these questions in writing, in advance of the interview as well as in person. The same interviewer (Sopory) conducted all of the interviews. After each interview, he created a written interview synopsis, which was then twice reviewed for accuracy and completeness by the interviewee. Final versions of all the synopses appear in Part III.

In our presentation of the interview findings, we include a brief biographical sketch of each interviewee before his or her interview. The questions that guided the interviews are reproduced in each interview (the first question is answered as part of the interviewee's biographical sketch). In a few cases, not all questions were answered by a given interviewee, so occasionally a question may be omitted from the sequence of items. While some editing of the original responses has been done, both by us and by the interviewees, we have attempted to maintain the flavor of the interviewees' original responses as much as possible.

(4) *Development of Generalizations.* We developed a comprehensive computerized data base containing the results of the literature review and the key informant interviews. We then clinically analyzed this data base—the elements of which are presented in the references and interview transcript sections of this book—to derive the generalizations presented in Part II.

(5) *Development of Summary for Substance Abuse Prevention and High-Risk Youth.* In addition, we analyzed the data base to provide an overview statement targeted to individuals and organizations providing substance abuse prevention-oriented services to high-risk youth. The full statement is provided in an executive summary for Backer et al. (1990); a brief summary of this statement follows.

Substance Abuse and High-Risk Youth

Alcohol and other drug use among high-risk youth is a special focus of this book for reasons already presented. Most experts agree that the key to reduction in substance abuse is *prevention*, and that the key to prevention lies in reaching America's youth. The focus on high-risk youth is a critical part, therefore, of the nation's overall effort to reduce substance abuse. In this section, we present a brief context for substance abuse prevention efforts targeted to high-risk youth, and in the next, a specific analysis of why and how drug abuse came to be such an important issue on the public agenda in 1986-1987. This analysis is important because we will return later to explore what our comparative synthesis findings *mean* for substance abuse mass media campaigns targeted to high-risk youth.

The Office for Substance Abuse Prevention was created by the Anti-Drug Abuse Act of 1986 to assist communities and organizations across the United States in developing various approaches to prevention, treatment, and rehabilitation through community-based model programs and other activities. Past research has shown that (a) almost no use of cigarettes, alcohol, or illicit drugs (except cocaine) begins after age 25; and (b) the number of youth with substance abuse experience is fairly considerable (64% of high school seniors used alcohol, 12% had used cocaine and 3.4% were current users; 2.7% used marijuana daily in the 1988 High School Seniors Survey of the National Institute on Drug Abuse).

Therefore, OSAP's efforts are aimed at influencing the attitudes and behavior of young people away from substance use. Young people who are particularly vulnerable or at "high risk" are a special high-priority audience: abused and neglected youngsters, the homeless or runaways, gateway drug (alcohol, tobacco, and marijuana) users, the physically or mentally disabled, pregnant teens, school dropouts, children of alcohol and other drug users, latchkey children, and economically disadvantaged youth.

A considerable amount of research has been done on adolescent substance abuse. This research shows that most such abuse (a) occurs in sequential stages, beginning usually with tobacco and progressing through marijuana and alcohol (the so-called gateway drugs), with some high-risk youth moving on to other illicit drugs; (b) has multiple causes, with risk for an adolescent's abuse increasing according to the number of risk factors he or she experiences; (c) serves multiple social-psychological functions in adolescents, with transition marking and social acceptance being especially salient in early adolescence; and (d) is a statistically normative experience in U.S. culture, with most youths maturing out of substance abuse. However, adolescent substance abuse tends to occur as part of a constellation of problem behaviors that are identifiable in childhood by antisocial behaviors.

All of these factors make it imperative for substance abuse prevention activities to occur in the "conscious context" of school, community, and peers—including the elements of society that present some ambivalence about substance use (e.g., federal subsidies for tobacco, legal use of alcohol). Increases in the numbers of high-risk youth—through increasing poverty, breakup of the nuclear family by decreasing divorces, and so on—also have an impact on the problem (Office for Substance Abuse Prevention, 1989).

Many of the campaign designers interviewed for this book have extensive experience in developing and conducting campaigns targeted to high-risk youth. Substance abuse prevention and other health topics have been the focus of these campaigns. Interviewees reinforced strongly the notion that campaigns must pay attention to the psychological realities of high-risk youth and the current demographic evidence about alcohol and drug abuse—many campaigns are designed and implemented without close examination of the realities they are trying to affect. For instance, campaign messages that highlight important themes in the development of adolescent identity—including freedom, autonomy, and peer group acceptance—have a greater likelihood of success, all other things being equal. Some of these themes are also reinforced in the literature examined for this study (and reviewed in our annotated bibliography; see Backer et al., 1991).

A summary of some important recommendations for structuring of health communication campaigns targeted to substance abuse prevention and high-risk youth are presented in Part II.

Setting the Agenda for the Issue of Drugs

The current social emphasis on substance abuse is related to larger social phenomena and to aspects of the mass media, which must be taken into account if we are to understand fully how mass media health campaigns in this topic area actually work. While there is by anyone's estimation a problem with abuse of street and prescription drugs in the United States, the "drug abuse crisis" of 1986 was not due to any sudden overall rise in drug use or the severity of its consequences (Kerr, 1986). In fact, drug use by high school seniors and by young people actually *declined* from 1981 to 1986 (most of the decline was in marijuana use, with cocaine use holding steady).

The causes do include the introduction into the United States of a new and potent form of cocaine called "crack" (Shoemaker, 1989). Crack is smoked instead of snorted, creating a more immediate and more intense effect on the individual. While crack had been used by some individuals in the United States for several years prior to 1986, at that time it began to be more widely used, especially by lower-income individuals, who were more likely to be minorities.

The June 1986 death of Len Bias, a young basketball star at the University of Maryland, in the Washington, D.C., area, as well as the approaching November 1986 elections, helped the U.S. Congress focus attention on the drug problem. Deeper trends having to do with an antidrug and antialcohol sentiment building among the U.S. public since the early 1980s, reflecting the end of the "tolerant" era of the late 1960s and the 1970s, provided a larger values context for the agenda-setting of drugs as a national priority in 1986.

Emphasis on the "drug issue" in the mass media also had an effect, as did the number of celebrities disclosing their problems with alcohol or drug addiction, beginning with Betty Ford in the early 1980s. The appearance of six *Time* magazine cover stories and many front-page *New York Times* articles on substance abuse helped to create public urgency for action and provided motivation for lawmakers to legislate solutions.

If fighting substance abuse in the United States is in part a matter of resetting values and refocusing attention, then mass media health behavior campaigns for substance abuse prevention need to be designed in ways that take advantage of that reality. The specific role that the mass media have played in elevating public attention about alcohol and drug abuse is important, including the extent to which media professionals and organizations may feel this is an "old issue" or that "message clutter" about drugs has begun to occur in entertainment, news, and public service programming. Such statements appeared in the pages of *Daily Variety* and other media trade publications beginning in 1988. Campaign designers must therefore be very careful when approaching media organizations or celebrities—for example, they should state up front why a particular campaign has elements that are not already "overdone" or "overexposed," and why it can contribute something unique.

THE AGENDA-SETTING PROCESS FOR THE ISSUE OF DRUGS

How did a social problem such as drug abuse rise to importance on the mass media agenda in the United States? What consequences result? One framework for analyzing such questions is that of the *agenda-setting process*, which has been studied by a number of social scientists. As defined by Rogers and Dearing (1988), among others, the agenda-setting process is a social phenomenon through which an issue (e.g., AIDS or the environmental crisis) begins to receive sharply increased mass media coverage, in turn creating more widespread public opinion about the issue, and eventually leading to responses by policymakers. The "marker" of the agenda-setting process is "newshole capacity" in the national media, which is charted for the drug abuse issue in Figure 3, showing dramatic spikes with certain critical events. Media coverage of the drug issue was measured by Merriam (1989) as the percentage of the newshole (the column inches of newspaper space devoted to news—that is, other than advertising space). Anthony Downs (1972) argues

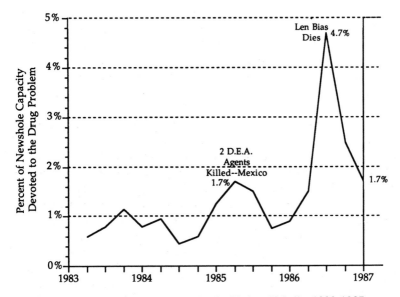

Figure 3. Coverage of the Drug Issue in the National Media, 1982-1987
SOURCE: Merriam (1989). Used by permission.

that this rise and fall typifies the agenda-setting process for most issues. The process and its critical components are depicted in Figure 4.

    The history of the issue of drug abuse in the United States provides a fascinating illustration of the agenda-setting process. It has not followed a typical agenda-setting pattern, in which an issue usually follows an up-and-down sequence on the national agenda over a period of months or years. The drug issue is unique in that since its rise it has maintained a rather prominent place on the national agenda. Further, *the drug issue rose and fell on the national agenda somewhat independently of the "real-world indicators" of the U.S. drug problem, such as the number of drug users or the number of drug-related deaths per year.* Analyzing the agenda-setting process for 10 different issues during the period from 1945 to 1980 (which includes the 1973 "war on drugs"), Neuman (1990) concludes that drugs represent a "symbolic crisis," in which the media, the public, and the U.S. government define an issue as a crisis for a limited period of time. According to Neuman, the public agenda is typically less responsive to media coverage of a symbolic crisis than to coverage of a real crisis.

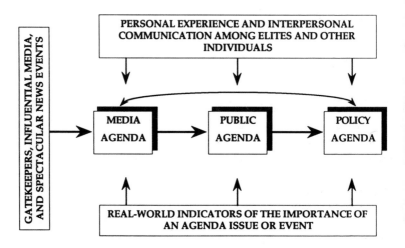

Figure 4. Three Main Components in the Agenda-Setting Process: The Media Agenda, the Public Agenda, and the Policy Agenda
SOURCE: Rogers and Dearing (1988).

A somewhat similar case of agenda-setting without an increase in real-world indicators is that of drunk driving in the 1980s. "The anti-drunk driving movement did not spring from any rise in the incidence or prevalence of drinking-driving or in accidents thought to be related to it" (Reinarman, 1988). Instead, the issue of drunken driving was put on the national agenda almost solely through the efforts of one organization, Mothers Against Drunk Driving (MADD), which was founded by Candy Lightner of Sacramento in 1980 when her daughter was killed by a drunken driver. Within eight years, the anti-drunken driver movement had attracted tremendous media coverage and considerable public attention (a 1984 national poll found that 85% recognized the name MADD) and had achieved such policy accomplishments as passage of legislation for a nationwide minimum drinking age of 21, for reducing the blood alcohol content standard for drunken driving from .10% to .08% or even .05%, and more frequent highway sobriety checkpoints to stop vehicles randomly (Reinarman, 1988).

Another analysis demonstrating the irrelevance of real-world indicators to agenda-setting is the issue of AIDS. In the United States from 1981, when the epidemic began, to 1985, when it finally began to receive media attention, the number of AIDS cases reported to the

Centers for Disease Control rose steadily. The epidemic did not achieve a place on the media agenda until (a) Rock Hudson was diagnosed with AIDS, and (b) Ryan White, a young Indiana boy with AIDS, was banned from school attendance (Rogers et al., 1991).

MEDIA COVERAGE OF THE DRUG PROBLEM

Adam Weisman (1986), a Washington journalist, states in an article titled "I Was a Drug-Hype Junkie": "For a reporter at a national news organization in 1986, the drug crisis in America is more than a story, it's an addiction—and a dangerous one." Why and how did the drug problem suddenly command so much media attention in 1986? Both *The New York Times* and the White House helped set the media agenda. *The New York Times* assigned a reporter to cover illegal drugs full-time in November 1985, shortly after the Reverend Jesse Jackson visited A. M. Rosenthal, then the paper's executive director, to discuss this issue. *The New York Times* carried its first front-page story on crack on November 29, 1985 (Kerr, 1986). When the *Times* considers an issue newsworthy, many other U.S. media are influenced to follow suit (Rogers et al., 1991).

On the basis of his analysis of the agenda-setting process for the drug problem, Merriam (1989) concludes: "National media coverage of drug issues between 1983 and 1987 followed a classic pattern: There was a slow initial increase in overall media attention, followed by a shift in emphasis to subject matters of broader interest. Then interest [that is, media coverage] in drugs increased sharply, peaked, and declined" (p. 21).

The media responded to the death of Len Bias and to White House influences with what Reinarman and Levine (1989, p. 115) call a "crack attack," with much of the coverage dealing with the new, more dangerous form of ingesting cocaine by smoking it. Actually, crack was not new in the United States: "Politicians and the media focussed attention on crack *not* because the cocaine was ingested in a more direct, dangerous manner, for this had been going on for years. Rather, their attention focussed on the new downward mobility and increased visibility of cocaine in the form of crack" (Reinarman & Levine, 1989, p. 117).

Media coverage of crack in 1986 was a kind of "feeding frenzy." *Time* devoted five 1986 cover stories to the crack crisis. CBS News with anchor Dan Rather broadcast the two-hour documentary *48 Hours on Crack Street*. The media used such words as *crisis, plague,* and *epidemic* to describe the drug problem in the United States (Reinarman & Levine, 1989, p. 118).

The Associated Press annual survey of editors rated "new efforts to combat drug addiction" as the ninth most important news story of 1986. This was the only year in the decade of the 1980s when the drug problem was rated in the top 10 news stories of the year.

OBJECTIVE INDICATORS OF THE DRUG PROBLEM

How important are drug abuse deaths relative to other types of substance abuse? In 1985, cocaine use led to 613 overdose deaths, while alcohol contributed to about 100,000 deaths (Weisman, 1986). Put another way: "For every *one* cocaine-related death in the U.S. in 1987, there were approximately 300 tobacco-related deaths and 100 alcohol-related deaths" (Reinarman & Levine, 1989, p. 120). Further, many of these cocaine-related deaths were not due to crack, although this more dangerous way of ingesting cocaine rose to media attention in 1986.

The media and the White House focused on young people as the main population at risk for cocaine abuse. However, the National Institute on Drug Abuse (NIDA) national surveys of more than 8,000 U.S. households showed that the percentage of 18- to 25-year-olds who had ever tried cocaine peaked in 1982, four years prior to the drug crisis of 1986 (Reinarman & Levine, 1989). The number of high school seniors who said they had tried cocaine peaked in 1982, and then stabilized or declined thereafter. On the basis of these and other data, Reinarman and Levine (1989) conclude: "The trends in official drug use statistics had been downward, not upward, even before the scare began" (p. 121).

PUBLIC OPINION ON THE DRUG PROBLEM

Did the extensive media coverage of the drug problem influence public opinion? Using data from Gallup polls, Shoemaker, Wanta, and Leggett (1989) found that the percentage of the American public saying that drugs were "the most important problem facing America today" in 43 different polls from 1972 to 1986 was correlated with the amount of media coverage given to the drug issue a few months prior to the poll.

An April 1986 national poll sponsored by *The New York Times*/CBS News found that 2% of American adults considered drugs to be the nation's most important problem. Five months later, in August 1986, following the media coverage of the death of Len Bias, 13% of American adults said that drugs were the nation's most important problem

(Kerr, 1986). By June-July 1989, a Gallup poll found that 27% of adults said that drugs were the most important problem.

An earlier "drug crisis" had been perceived by the American public in 1973, when as many as 20% of the adults participating in a Gallup poll said that drug abuse was the most important national problem. Two years later, in 1975, the proportion had dropped from 20% to zero (Beniger, 1983). Here we see an example of the rise-and-fall nature of the public agenda-setting process for the drug issue.

FEDERAL RESPONSE TO THE DRUG PROBLEM

Recent years have seen increasing federal government involvement in combating the drug problem in the United States. The National Institute on Drug Abuse was created in 1974, partly as a response to the 1973 "crisis." In the 1980s, NIDA launched a major campaign aimed at young teenagers and their parents, called Just Say No. First Lady Nancy Reagan played an important role in this campaign. Television public service announcements (PSAs) were played 1,150 times per month by a sample of television stations that were monitored. Notice that Nancy Reagan's involvement as an antidrug crusader began well before the 1986 drug crisis. Reinarman and Levine (1989, p. 127) argue that Nancy Reagan's involvement in fighting drugs was a public relations move to counter the public criticism in the early 1980s of her expensive evening gowns and the hundreds of thousands of dollars she spent for new china for the White House while national unemployment rates were relatively high.

Then, beginning in April 1986, NIDA launched another campaign called Cocaine: The Big Lie, which was aimed at adults. The campaign's PSAs were played from 1,500 to 2,500 times per month by the typical television station in the United States.

In 1986, the Office for Substance Abuse Prevention was created, with a main objective of preventing alcohol and other drug use by America's young people. While NIDA mainly conducts research on drugs, OSAP carries out preventive campaigns.

On October 17, 1986, the Anti-Drug Abuse Act, the most far-reaching drug law ever passed by the U.S. Congress, was approved by a vote of 392 to 16. This law increased federal funding for law enforcement and for drug treatment and education programs (Kerr, 1986). The act was passed just prior to the fall 1986 elections. "The prominence of the drug issue dropped sharply in both political speeches and media coverage after the 1986 election, only to return during the 1988 election year"

(Reinarman & Levine, 1989, p. 129). Then, just prior to the 1988 election, Congress passed an even stricter and more costly antidrug bill. During the 1988 presidential election campaign, both of the candidates emphasized the grave nature of the drug problem, and what they would do to solve it.

From 1981 to 1987, federal funding for antidrug law enforcement tripled, from $1 billion to $3 billion. An additional $5 billion was spent in 1987 by state and local law enforcement agencies, about one-fifth of their total budget (Nadelmann, 1989).

NIDA's annual budget went from $65 million in 1986 to $400 million in 1990. NIDA funds research on drug-related problems, although much of the increase in the institute's budget was in fact for study of a drug-related problem—HIV infection and AIDS. Total federal spending for all drug programs reached $10.6 billion in 1990, up from $6.3 billion in 1988.

Thus the agenda-setting process for the drug issue in the late 1980s can be characterized as one in which the issue climbed to a high priority on the media agenda, the public agenda, and the policy agenda, without an overall increase in real-world indicators of the drug problem.

PART TWO

Generalizations About
Health Communication Campaigns

Overview

Our research—an extensive literature review combined with 29 campaign designer interviews—identified 27 generalizations about what makes for effective health communication campaigns. While an emphasis has been placed throughout this study on mass media campaigns for substance abuse prevention and high-risk youth, these findings are *not* limited to substance abuse campaigns, but may be applied in other campaigns, perhaps with certain modifications.

These generalizations have a common construction—they speak of characteristics of "more effective" campaigns. No assumption is made that one characteristic is more important than another, or that any one is essential for success. The generalizations are derived from both empirical and analytic work, and were selected on the basis of their appearance in some fairly clear form in a number of works reviewed. No one source mentioned all 27. Applications of the 27 generalizations in research and practice are discussed in Part IV.

Generalizations About
Health Communication Campaigns

(1) More effective campaigns use multiple media (television, radio, print, and so on).

(2) More effective campaigns combine mass media with community, small group, and individual activities, supported by an existing community structure (this involves using a "systems approach" to campaigns).

(3) More effective campaigns carefully target or segment the audience that the campaign is intended to reach.

(4) Celebrities can attract public attention to a campaign issue. Public attention can be achieved by embedding a campaign's message in an entertainment program.

(5) Repetition of a single message makes for a more effective campaign.

(6) Campaigns for preventive behavior are more effective if they emphasize positive behavior change rather than the negative consequences of current behavior. Arousing fear is rarely successful as a campaign strategy.

(7) Campaigns are more effective if they emphasize current rewards rather than the avoidance of distant negative consequences.

(8) More effective campaigns involve in their design and operation key power figures and groups in mass media organizations and in government bodies.

(9) The timing of a campaign (when it is introduced, what else is happening during its operation, and the like) helps to determine campaign effectiveness.

(10) More effective campaigns utilize formative evaluation techniques to appraise and improve the campaigns during planning and while they are in operation.

(11) More effective campaigns set fairly modest, attainable goals in terms of behavior change.

(12) The use of commercial marketing and social marketing strategies has potential for increasing the effectiveness of campaigns.

(13) More effective campaigns utilize educational messages in entertainment contexts (this is called the education-entertainment strategy, and is discussed further in Part IV).

(14) More effective campaigns make deliberate efforts to resolve potential conflicts between evaluation researchers and message creators.

(15) More effective campaigns address the larger social-structural and environmental factors impinging on the health problems the campaigns are attempting to influence (e.g., poverty and lack of economic opportunity are related to substance abuse).

(16) More effective campaigns are coordinated with direct service delivery components (e.g., hot line numbers for information or counseling), so that immediate follow-through can take place if behavior change begins to occur.

(17) Segmentation of campaign audiences by demographics is often relatively ineffective, compared with segmentation by psychographic variables based upon attitudes, values, and beliefs.

(18) More effective campaigns direct messages to people linked to targeted individuals, especially individuals with direct interpersonal influence, such as peers and parents.

(19) More effective campaigns choose their positive role models for social learning carefully, as these individuals may become negative role models through their personal actions (e.g., celebrities involved in substance abuse campaigns who later are discovered to have substance abuse problems themselves).

(20) If fear appeals are used in campaign messages, they should be coupled with mechanisms for reducing the anxiety that is created.

(21) Public service announcements alone generally do not effectively bring about behavior change. PSAs should be combined with other campaign activities.

(22) More effective campaigns use the news media as a means of increasing their visibility.

(23) The role of the government in campaigns is mainly to provide (a) funding for campaign activities and (b) appropriate leadership on controversial issues.

(24) More effective campaigns address the existing knowledge and beliefs of target audiences that are impeding adoption of desired behaviors.

(25) More effective campaigns communicate incentives or benefits for adopting desired behaviors that build on the existing motives, needs, and values of target audiences.

(26) More effective campaigns focus target audiences' attention on immediate, high-probability consequences of healthy behavior.

(27) More effective campaigns use pretesting to ensure that campaign messages have the expected effects on target audiences.

Discussion

Two concepts presented in these generalizations may require further explanation. *Social marketing* is an approach to directed change that is intended to increase the acceptability of new ideas to target audiences by applying marketing strategies adapted from commercial marketing to social issues, such as improved health, adult literacy, and contraception (Lefebvre & Flora, 1988). Strategies of social marketing include (a) audience segmentation, (b) consumer orientation, (c) using formative evaluation research methods (including pretesting), and (d) the use of symbols.

Bandura (1986) first proposed the concepts of *social learning theory*, a perspective that has been widely used in recent health communication campaigns. The basic idea of social learning is that individuals learn by observing individual models who perform particular behaviors. The models may be in everyday life, or they may be depicted in the mass media. For instance, until recent years, prime-time television series in the United States often showed characters doing a great deal of gratuitous drinking of alcohol. Today, in an era of heightened awareness about alcoholism, the television industry has eliminated most drinking that does not contribute directly to a program's story line. It is hoped that the removal of drinking scenes will diminish the modeling of alcohol-related behavior by audiences. Thus we see that social modeling may be unplanned and spontaneous. Many media campaigns for health today seek to utilize social learning theory in a purposive way. For instance, the designated driver concept was depicted in more than 35 different prime-time television shows in 1988-1989. As a result, many Americans learned about the designated driver idea, and many people used it.

Entertainment-education soap operas and related strategies (see Part IV) generally provide positive role models for the health behavior being promoted. The positive role models should be attractive to the audience, and should be rewarded for their positive behavior in the soap opera story line. Negative role models are usually also depicted, and are punished for their "bad" behavior.

SUBSTANCE ABUSE AND HIGH-RISK YOUTH

Following are some additional generalizations that emerged from our research that are specific to the design of health communication campaigns for substance abuse prevention with high-risk youth. Many other specific target audiences also have been the subjects of campaigns, and analyses of campaigns for the same audience with different behavior topics might be useful for these groups as well.

(1) *Campaigns for substance abuse prevention should start at grades 5 and 6, when children are aged 11 or 12.* "Reminder campaigns" then can be conducted as these children grow into adolescence. Past research shows that substantial numbers of youth begin substance use/abuse by junior high school, so prevention-oriented campaigns must start before that time. Campaigns that focus on "gateway drugs"—alcohol, tobacco, and marijuana—are especially likely to have long-term impacts.

(2) *Campaigns for substance abuse prevention should include efforts to increase awareness of the broader social contexts in which substance abuse occurs.* For example, campaigns might include student debates about tobacco and alcohol advertising in the media and the use of promotions targeted to minority adolescents.

(3) *Campaigns for substance abuse prevention among high-risk youth should include educational messages to parents.* For example, such campaigns should encourage parents to talk with their children about drugs and should work with parent groups that sponsor drug-free parties.

(4) *Campaigns for substance abuse prevention among high-risk youth should use messages that highlight important themes in the development of adolescent identity, including freedom, autonomy, and peer group acceptance.* Substance use often occurs in response to events that

involve these powerful themes. Prevention campaigns can highlight coping skills for "saying no," and can emphasize how to resist pressures from advertisers or substance-using peers. Presenting older peers who display such skills can provide positive role models.

(5) *Campaigns for substance abuse prevention among high-risk youth should use peer models, rather than celebrity adults, as campaign spokespersons.* Rebellious youth may view any adult spokesperson with suspicion.

(6) *Campaigns for substance abuse prevention among high-risk youth should include "image" or "life-style" advertising to promote an active, healthy life-style that is by its nature intolerant of substance use.* Such healthy life-style strategies have worked well for many commercial products.

(7) *Campaigns for substance abuse prevention among high-risk youth should use radio as a communication channel.* Radio is a relatively low-cost medium to use, and it plays an important role in the everyday lives of young people.

PART THREE

Interviews With
Campaign Designers/Experts

Following are 29 interviews, presented in alphabetical order according to interviewees' last names. A standard format is used: Each interview is introduced with the respondent's name and primary organizational affiliation, a brief preamble states the interviewee's background and experience in mass media health campaigns, and a narrative summary of the interview follows.

All of the interviewees have had experience in designing campaigns, directly or indirectly. They include campaign scholars who have helped to shape campaigns and media professionals who do work that is included in campaigns.

While we edited these interviews for coherence, structure, and brevity, our intent was to preserve the flavor of the interviewees' words as much as possible. Thus colloquial expressions and interrupted trains of thought have been left intact. Each interviewee twice reviewed his or her interview for accuracy and completeness.

ELAINE BRATIC ARKIN
Georgetown University

ABOUT THE INTERVIEWEE

Elaine Bratic Arkin has more than 20 years' experience in developing and managing health-related communications programs for public, patient, and health professional audiences. She has planned, developed, and managed national mass media campaigns on such topics as cigarette smoking, asbestos awareness, substance abuse prevention, cancer, and prenatal care.

In addition to mass media programs, Arkin was responsible for developing a national toll-free telephone counseling service promoted through the media (the Cancer Information Service) and a national coalition (the Healthy Mothers, Healthy Babies Coalition) to improve communication within the maternal and child health community. Each of these programs has now survived for more than a decade.

In several governmental policy positions, including that of Deputy Assistant Secretary for the U.S. Department of Health and Human Services, Arkin developed and administered policies and standards related to the use of the mass media and public affairs functions.

Ms. Arkin serves as a consultant to approximately two dozen national public health and voluntary agencies, advising about communications planning, market research and strategic planning, evaluation, and communications-related research. Client issues with which she has been involved include AIDS, alcohol and other drug abuse prevention, smoking, Alzheimer's disease, cancer prevention, coalition building, "hard-to-reach" audiences, hypertension, infant and prenatal care, lupus, glaucoma, nutrition, pesticides, prescription drug use, risk communication, toxic substances, and water pollution.

Ms. Arkin has authored a number of articles and publications related to planning and evaluating health and risk communications programs. She is author of *Making Health Communications Work: A Planner's Guide* (National Cancer Institute, 1989).

*   *   *

What are the most common reasons mass media campaigns do not achieve their hoped-for results, and what are the most common reasons some campaigns are relatively successful?

Most campaigns have overly optimistic time schedules, and do not devote enough time to planning and to research, and to distribution and marketing. Campaign managers generally think that a campaign ends with the production of campaign messages. Less attention is given to a good marketing strategy. A common characteristic of unsuccessful campaigns is the underestimation of the costs required to develop and carry out the complex activities that are required. In general, successful campaigns are long term and are designed so that midterm corrections can be made.

Unfortunately, an important factor in a campaign's success is how exciting or how "hot" the topic is in the media's eyes and in public opinion. So the timing of a campaign is important: A campaign has to be implemented at the right time, by the right people, having the right connections. To some extent, this favorable environment can be created where it does not naturally exist.

How could present health communication campaign models be improved to make them useful for planning, implementing, and evaluating mass media campaigns?

There are a lot of usable models for public communication campaigns, but the translation of these models into working methods is a particular problem. There is not much need to change basic campaign models, but more work is required to teach people how to *use* the models in practical ways that fit with real-world limitations—resources, politics, personalities, and so forth.

What roles can formative or summative evaluation play in the relative success of a health communication campaign?

Formative evaluation and the use of focus groups are helpful, but there is a danger of drawing whatever conclusion one wants to draw from the data collected! Conclusions from qualitative research can be misleading. Focus groups should be analyzed by people who have a great deal of experience with this method, and the conclusions should be backed up with quantitative research where possible. We also should look at national polls and at past studies of campaigns, and *then* come back to use focus groups in a supplementary way. The problem is that too often a few focus groups are considered sufficient formative research, which is rarely true.

Summative evaluation is useful for planning future campaigns, and, more important, for disseminating data about the effects of a campaign.

However, some sort of tracking evaluation should be constantly going on during a media campaign to permit adjustments where needed.

What are the unique characteristics and special difficulties of preventive health communication campaigns, especially those aimed at high-risk youth?

The conditions that turn high-risk youth to using drugs are important to consider. We have to understand the social problems in order to find out why kids take drugs in the first place, before we create drug abuse prevention campaigns. Drug-related problems of youth typically have much deeper roots than what communication messages deal with. We should not look for superficial answers to serious problems. Some high-risk youth have no hope, live in poverty, have troubles at home, and have problems fitting in with society. Peer pressure and social nonacceptance will not work as communication strategies if the drugs are, in effect, "fixing" some sort of problem for these children, even if the fixing has potentially lethal side effects.

Drugs for high-risk youth "take them out" of their lives. Drug abuse is a societal problem, and as communicators our duty is to be advocates for social change. The alternatives for high-risk youth lie in new services and not just in communication about individual behavior change.

How do factors such as age groupings, fear appeals, audience segmentation, and use of opinion leaders contribute to the design of mass media campaigns targeted to high-risk youth?

We should ask researchers for help in determining what age groups to target in media campaigns, but we must use caution when targeting campaign activities by chronological age. Audience segmentation is crucial, but we must incorporate more psychographic research and developmental factors in segmentation decisions. Age is only a shortcut answer.

More research is needed on the use of fear appeals. Fear may be helpful for achieving short-term objectives, but not for long-term effects, as are required for drug abuse prevention. On the other hand, kids love scary stuff, and their perception of fear may be very different from that of adults. Thus some kinds of fear appeals may actually be successful with young audiences.

Using opinion leaders may not work for high-risk youth. To find out, we must ask them about their preferences and spend a lot of time talking to them, to gather data for use in campaign design.

The choice of communication channels depends on the message and the audience, but generally we lack control over the channels—at least in terms of what is done with the message once it is distributed (e.g., a TV public service announcement, which a TV network agrees to air, but it shows up only in early-morning telecasts so that its audience is very limited). Usually, the more communication channels used in a campaign, the more potentially effective the campaign, but there is a danger in using an ineffective channel just because it is available.

Mass communication methods can be used best for attention getting and for conveying new information. For skills building, community channels (including schools) are more effective.

What is the most successful mass media campaign to change health behavior you have known, and why do you think it worked?

A high blood pressure prevention campaign in America has been very successful, and has endured for almost 20 years. It has never been just a media campaign, but always has had a community outreach component. There also has been a tie-in with pharmaceutical companies and the medical care system that has enabled the tracking of patients and campaign progress.

What role should federal, state, or local governments play in media campaigns?

Guidelines and strategies for campaigns should be developed at the national level by the federal government or other national agencies. State and local agencies should seek to identify campaigns relevant to their needs, and to modify existing campaign materials, where possible, to suit particular issues, rather than to develop totally new materials, as media materials are expensive to produce.

What organizations and organizational factors contribute to the success or failure of media campaigns?

No one is in favor of drugs (as opposed to alcohol), and so for television networks, which serve as gatekeepers, there should not be any problem in airing drug-related campaign messages. Television networks should be included as more active partners in campaigns on topics such as drug abuse, for which more national attention to solutions (not just problems) is still needed. In some cases, for example, networks have developed issue-specific campaigns, devoting far more corporate energy and airtime than we generally expect them to contribute.

With the Ad Council, the ability to choose an advertising agency is curtailed and control over campaign design can be lost, even while incurring costs (although the Ad Council provides volunteer services, direct costs are charged to the client). Advocacy groups can help advance an issue, but they should be distant partners in a media campaign because their role is to highlight issues and create controversy.

What methods would you suggest for financing media campaigns for health?

Corporate sponsorship is a good way of raising funds for media campaigns, and can be utilized more than it is at present. Also, campaign materials already produced, if they are good, should be utilized again after suitable modifications. Public service announcements and other materials often are offered only once, and are rarely used to a message "wear-out" point. Opportunities for cost sharing with other agencies, the original producer of a campaign, the federal government, and local communities should be looked into for cost savings and time savings as well.

WARREN J. ASHLEY
Entertainment Industry Coalition on AIDS

ABOUT THE INTERVIEWEE

Warren J. Ashley was the Program Policy Manager at the National Broadcasting Company for such series as *The A-Team, Golden Girls,* and *Miami Vice* from 1982 to 1988. Prior to that time, he was an Instructor in Teacher Education and Child Development and Program Development Specialist and Community Liaison for the Teacher Corps Project at California State University, Fullerton. His experience also includes community mental health administration, child and family counseling and consultation to schools, police departments, and public agencies. He has had direct contact with high-risk youth through his experience in teaching at a continuation high school and in working as a community mental health counselor.

Dr. Ashley is a member of the Center for Population Options Media Advisory Board and Chairman of the Entertainment Industry Coalition on AIDS, which is involved with the accurate and responsible portrayal of AIDS in the media. He received his B.A. degree in history and an M.A. degree in education at California State University, Los Angeles, and his Ph.D. in education from Claremont Graduate School. From 1965 to 1968, he served in the Peace Corps as an elementary school teacher, administrator, and community worker in Monrovia, Liberia.

* * *

What are the most common reasons mass media campaigns do not achieve their hoped-for results, and what are the most common reasons some campaigns are relatively successful?

Different people have different definitions of "success" for mass media health campaigns. In fact, defining success is often quite problematic: Is it the number of public service announcements (PSAs) produced, the number of times a PSA gets aired, the number of times automobile seat belts are worn on the television screen, use or nonuse of alcohol on the television screen, the change in attitude of the viewers, or the actual behavior change of viewers? If success is defined as the number of PSAs aired or as the change in behavior portrayed on the television screen, then a reason for success is a matter of being persistent with the television networks. For the American television networks actually to make a change in broadcasting practice (e.g., airing condom PSAs or ads), you have to just keep hammering away; coolly, politely, without threatening, just inundating them with letters, talks, and so on.

The effectiveness of PSAs is open to question. Apart from making organizations feel they have achieved something and completed their responsibilities, and thus can skip making some hard decisions, PSAs are good primarily for creating awareness, and are not useful for changing attitudes and behavior.

Experience with children and television shows that the media intrinsically are a very powerful influence on people's attitudes but typically *not* on their behavior, because changing behavior requires that people give up something that is giving them pleasure, and substitute for it another behavior that gives less pleasure or no pleasure. This is especially true of drug abuse and practicing safe sex to prevent AIDS. No matter how much the mass media try to change attitudes or behavior, change boils down to a "pleasure/pain" principle and the majority of people are going to opt for pleasure. *What media can do is to prepare the soil for someone else to seed.*

How could present health communication campaign models be improved to make them useful for planning, implementing, and evaluating mass media campaigns?

If there were a media campaign that was somehow connected to an actual one-on-one contact with the audience, and the direct contact was done in a way that was considered credible and meaningful by the target audience, there might be some significant results. For example, community colleges would be a very good way to reach adolescents. A conference of youth opinion leaders might be called, and these youth could become resources for AIDS prevention information, so that they could go into their groups to spread the word. Without personal contact, there is little chance for success of a media campaign in terms of changing actual behavior.

Most of the current media campaigns just make the people conducting them feel better! The campaigns provide them with the illusion that something is being accomplished. The choices of the people who go into the community are often absurd, like middle-aged persons, or outstanding white middle-class college kids. High-risk youth do not listen to these kinds of people.

Information about drugs, AIDS, and the like is definitely getting out, but it is not getting to the right people, and not getting out in ways that are meaningful and credible to high-risk youth. From observation and the resulting health statistics it seems that this information is not affecting the target audience we most want to reach.

What roles can formative or summative evaluation play in the relative success of a health communication campaign?

Usually evaluation is done in terms of what happened. Evaluation obviously can play an important part, if it is a legitimate measurement of the people in the target audience that the campaign intends to impact. Evaluation carried out immediately after a message is communicated has some value, but the most valuable evaluation is done over time. Long-term tracking is seldom done, usually because of the lack of adequate money for evaluation, but that is the best method for determining campaign effects.

What you obtain from the evaluation information process is not nearly as important as the process of evaluation itself, if the objective of behavior change is seen as having precedence over the quality of the data collected. *We should utilize the process of evaluation itself as a mechanism for producing behavior change in a high-risk audience.* This way of creating behavior change is possible because the repeated interpersonal contact of the evaluator heightens and reinforces the campaign messages geometrically—*if* the evaluator knows *how* to do this.

People usually enter into evaluation research with some preconceptions. They conduct evaluations in ways that help their preconceptions to be validated. Evaluation can play an important role if it helps to structure a media campaign in a way that is more meaningful to the target audience. Formative evaluation of campaigns is good for planning, but if there were some way of involving youth directly in planning for the evaluation itself, campaigns would be better.

What are the unique characteristics and special difficulties of preventive health communication campaigns, especially those aimed at high-risk youth?

Young people believe they are invulnerable. They think they are the first people on earth to experience life. And, to be truthful, often young people will say things that you want to hear if it serves their purpose, or say things that you don't want to hear if that serves their purpose. My experience with teaching adolescents says that reaching a level where the adolescent will be honest, forthright, and in a position to self-disclose is extremely difficult. Young people constantly feel that "the world is against them." With high-risk youth, these troublesome characteristics are multiplied many times over. Another aspect of high-risk youth is that many of them are mobile, and it may be difficult to track their behavior over time.

How do factors such as age groupings, fear appeals, audience segmentation, and use of opinion leaders contribute to the design of mass media campaigns targeted to high-risk youth?

Experience and observation shows that the 9 to 12 age group seems to be the wrong target group for antidrug messages, as in the Just Say No campaign, because the inoculation does not last through the turbulence of puberty. The sweet kids of 11 to 12 years of age turn into "monsters" at 13 to 14 years. It is a biological change; it has everything to do with hormones and little to do with media campaigns. On the other hand, the group at 18 to 21 years may be the most receptive, as they are already past the negative parts of adolescence, and are concerned about adulthood. Prevention message effectiveness also depends on what is being taught to a kid. It might be more useful to teach children about being responsible, and to show them the relationship between behavior and the consequences likely to follow from their actions, than to just talk about drugs.

Antidrug PSAs produced in the early 1970s utilized a lot of fear appeals. These PSAs were effective for youth in non-high-risk situations, who would not have gone into high-risk situations anyway. Kids who were determined to "live hard and die young" were unaffected, and their intentions might even have been reinforced by such PSAs.

For message effectiveness, we must ensure that information is delivered to the target audience through groups they are comfortable with, and in groups that already exist, such as those in local neighborhoods. This, of course, goes beyond what mass media can do without local community involvement.

If the message is in the program content itself, then as long as one stays true to that program, the audience is already there. There is a group of musicians called Musicians for Life who have produced PSAs that are shown on MTV. The group uses popular rock musicians who have credibility (in a generic sense) with adolescents in the PSAs. To ensure diversity, and so that there is something for everyone, rock musicians from groups of different styles and cultural/ethnic backgrounds are used. Thus these PSAs address the different audience subsegments in the target audience of adolescents.

One way to identify "opinion leaders" is to look for people who are already breaking out in some way, for example, the student who might be doing better than the rest in a drafting class. These young people may have credibility both in the schools and out on the streets. They may also be able to communicate better than other youth with adults who are trying to effect health behavior change. We have to be looking for conduits to the target community who have credibility in both worlds.

Money is a good incentive—in our society, money talks. Money is valued, and so things that cost are good incentives. For example, the economic incentive of giving bus passes or parking permits to people attending an information session works because it makes them feel valued. Disincentives get back to fear appeals, threats, and coercion, which may produce only an appearance of change and no long-term change.

Television is effective for changing attitudes, and even more so if one is able to get messages included in existing programs. PSAs are a waste of money unless they are unique, like the Musicians for Life PSAs using rock musicians. Special programs such as the dedicated quiz programs, *How Much Do You Know About Home Burglary?* might also be effective because they present information in an entertaining way. Such programs are sometimes able to impart information that would not get through otherwise.

Radio as a medium for campaigns is underutilized. There certainly is not enough research being done on its effects today. Follow-up seems to be more difficult with radio, and this might be another reason for its underutilization.

What is the most successful mass media campaign to change health behavior you have known, and why do you think it worked?

Seat belt use campaigns have been among the most successful in terms of actually modifying behavior through portrayals and messages on television. The main reason for this is that what people are giving up to adopt seat belt use is not in itself pleasurable, and is not a big deal compared with drugs, AIDS, and so on, which require a lot of effort and pleasure denial.

What role should federal, state, or local governments play in media campaigns?

The federal and state governments seem to be very unrealistic about how the mass media operate, and especially about how the entertainment industry works. Local governments are more likely to know their own community. It is essential to work through a local government in order to get an appropriate message to the appropriate segment of the target population in local communities. The proper role of state and federal government is to provide funding to local governments for the conduct of such campaigns at the grass-roots level.

What organizations and organizational factors contribute to the success or failure of media campaigns?

Television networks and other large media organizations are businesses, and they tend to appreciate people who can relate to them on their own level. Media campaigns thus need to include people who can communicate effectively with these organizations.

What methods would you suggest for financing media campaigns for health?

It would be a better idea to spend the available resources for media campaigns more wisely. For example, the federal mailing of an AIDS brochure to 17 million people in 1989 was a sheer waste of money. The same money could have been spent more usefully in some other type of campaign.

CHARLES ATKIN
Michigan State University

ABOUT THE INTERVIEWEE

Charles Atkin is a Professor in the Departments of Communication and Telecommunications at Michigan State University and has been a Visiting Scholar at the Annenberg School for Communication, University of Southern California, and at the Department of Communication, Stanford University. He is an editor and contributing author of *Public Communication Campaigns* (Sage, 1989) and coauthor, with Lawrence Wallack, of *Mass Communication and Public Health: Complexities and Conflicts* (Sage, 1990). He has also written articles for a number of professional journals, such as *Journal of Adolescent Health Care, Journal of Studies on Alcohol, Journal of Communication,* and *Journal of Drug Education.*

Dr. Atkin has served on the editorial boards for *Communication Monographs, Human Communication Research, Journalism Quarterly, Journal of Broadcasting, Journal of Communication,* and *Psychology and Marketing.* He has also participated in a number of research projects, including Media Effects on Alcohol Consumption Patterns, sponsored by the Alcoholic Beverage Medical Research Foundation, Johns Hopkins University; and Prevention of Teenage Drinking and Driving, funded by the U.S. Department of Transportation and Michigan Office of Highway Safety Planning and Substance Abuse Services.

Dr. Atkin received his Ph.D. in mass communication from the University of Wisconsin in 1971.

*   *   *

What are the most common reasons mass media campaigns do not achieve their hoped-for results, and what are the most common reasons some campaigns are relatively successful?

At the high school level, drinking is a widespread phenomenon. About 70% of young people drink, and many drink excessively. Media campaigns have not been aimed at teenagers directly, because for them drinking is a positive cost-benefit trade-off: The perceived rewards are greater than the costs. Consequently, to influence teens to drink less or not to drink and drive is extremely difficult. So the campaigns stress interpersonal influences through parents and peers who are in a position to exercise "means control."

The single most important problem with media campaigns is the lack of compelling incentives in the campaign messages. The messages are narrow in the range of arguments they present, usually only saying what to do. They use often-repeated fear appeals. The point, usually lost on the creative people in ad agencies, is to come up with a persuasive appeal that will motivate the audience. Campaign professionals are so close to the arguments that they lose the perspective of the target audience, and so fall back on stereotypes.

There is a tendency to see what other campaigns on the same topic have done, and to use these other campaigns as models. This tendency limits the effectiveness of a campaign because each situation and each target audience is unique, even though some transfer learning certainly is possible.

The positioning of the messages in the media has also fallen into a pattern of television PSA, then radio PSA, and then magazine advertisements. There are many other potential channels of communication, such as place mats at McDonald's, or posters. Also, there are still new ways of exploiting television, such as putting PSAs in school TV broadcasts.

How could present health communication campaign models be improved to make them useful for planning, implementing, and evaluating mass media campaigns?

Messages should be made more attractive and engaging. Perhaps a bit of the substance of the message may be sacrificed in order to make the style more appealing. Adapting a message to the audience's knowledge level and preexisting values is important, since changing values is very difficult. We must try to change beliefs first, and then relate to values. This strategy requires formative research, but not just for the sake of doing focus groups or other formative evaluation research, as this is routinely carried out.

Different theories should be used at different stages of a campaign, or a combination of elements from different theoretical approaches should be used at an appropriate place. Most campaigns can use the "hierarchy of effects" model in designing the campaigns and their evaluation.

What roles can formative or summative evaluation play in the relative success of a health communication campaign?

Summative evaluation is too global and it usually does not single out key factors in campaign success. There is a tendency simply to *measure* behavior change in media campaign evaluations, rather than to find out what *caused* the change that was observed. The members of the target audience should be asked what caused them to change their health behaviors, so that some clues for future campaigns can be provided.

What are the unique characteristics and special difficulties of preventive health communication campaigns, especially those aimed at high-risk youth?

The value system of youth is very different from that of adults. What they are looking for in life is different from what is advocated in the arguments presented in most preventive health messages. Most of the message arguments do not pertain to, and are not relevant to, youth in the near future. At the age of 10 to 12 years, most kids become skeptical of authority and denigrate the sources of media messages. For a youth, the death of a friend from a drug overdose or drunk driving often has little effect.

How do factors such as age groupings, fear appeals, audience segmentation, and use of opinion leaders contribute to the design of mass media campaigns targeted to high-risk youth?

Campaigns targeted at younger kids can have large effects, but the effects will not last when the circumstances around the child change, as he or she grows up and cognitive development takes place. Campaigns can be most effective if targeted at the age group of 14 to 15 years.

Fear appeals based on the possibility of injury and death generally are not effective in media campaigns. In contrast, fear of rejection, fear of social embarrassment, and fear of getting caught by parents all have more potential for effect. Fear appeals should be looked at using the "protection paradigm," which distinguishes between *likelihood* and *seriousness*. Most fear appeals focus on seriousness. But high-probability, high-likelihood fear appeals of undetectable consequences will be more effective. For example, at the social level the fear appeal that if you drink, people are going to silently disapprove of you behind your back and not tell you openly about it will be effective; creation of paranoia will be effective!

Audience segmentation is difficult for media campaigns. Segmentation by age occurs naturally, but to break down the audience again, by gender, for example, is difficult.

Young females are more responsive than males to altruistic appeals to prevent their boyfriends, and other peers, from destructive activities. People who can exercise real influence over the target audience should be targeted by media campaigns.

For youth, television is losing its hold, and print is not an effective medium, except perhaps magazines for women. Radio is largely underutilized. We should develop alternative communication channels such as direct mail, bumper stickers, and signs to hang at parties.

About 70% of the mass media messages should be directed at significant others, rather than directly at the youth themselves. This strategy should be *planned*, rather than just hoping it will happen, in order to initiate a two-step flow of mass-interpersonal communication.

In general the following characteristics of a campaign message contribute to its success: an engaging style and content; high credibility as perceived by the audience; a high degree of immediate, concrete, explicit relevance of the message to the audience; compelling social, psychological, physical, and positive incentives; no stress on the disadvantages, by playing up the advantages of *not* engaging in the risky behavior; and, most important, a high-quality message. Also, the receptivity and the responsiveness of the audience to the campaign issue is important. For example, the success of the antilittering and antismoking campaigns has been partly due to the responsiveness of the audience to the idea for this type of behavior change.

What role should federal, state, or local governments play in media campaigns?

Government, the private sector, and in fact all concerned people as individuals should play a larger role in mass media health campaigns. The private sector should work more closely with government-funded campaigns in order to develop a meaningful partnership that combines the government's credibility and the private sector's finances. Campaign planning is best done at the federal level. Local and state agencies can modify campaign messages according to local needs.

What organizations and organizational factors contribute to the success or failure of media campaigns?

Advocacy groups are useful in energizing the government agencies involved in a campaign. Such groups can have impact, especially in the alcohol abuse and drug abuse areas, and the government should help them to do so by providing funding support. The Ad Council has the problem that it has to satisfy so many groups that their final products tend to be bland. The Ad Council does not take the task of a public service campaign as seriously as it does a commercial campaign in terms of looking aggressively for the most effective message strategy and insisting on using it. Television networks are responsive to pressures, as in their response to the designated driver campaign, but the problem is that their attention is short-lived—and no one issue will soon be replaced with another. More attention should be given to independent television stations, cable, and satellite distribution systems. Of all age groups, teenagers are most likely to diversify their viewing habits. Teenagers represent a fragmented audience, so *fragmented campaign strategies* must be used to reach them.

What methods would you suggest for financing media campaigns for health?

Private companies can be closely involved with antidrug campaigns, as there is no clash with commercial interests (as in the case of anti-alcohol projects). Financial resources from private companies should be explored further for funding future media campaigns.

THOMAS E. BACKER
Human Interaction Research Institute

ABOUT THE INTERVIEWEE

Thomas E. Backer is President of the Human Interaction Research Institute, a Los Angeles-based nonprofit center for research on knowledge utilization and planned change in health and human services, and on health communication. He is also Associate Clinical Professor of Medical Psychology at the UCLA School of Medicine.

Dr. Backer is the author of more than 250 books, articles, and research reports. His most recent books are *Drug Abuse Technology Transfer, Strategic Planning for Workplace Drug Abuse Programs* (2nd ed.) and *Organizational Change and Drug-Free Workplaces: Templates for Success* (with Kirk O'Hara). His recent articles focus on such subjects as mass media and health behavior, medical technology transfer, and creativity in the workplace. He has written widely about mass media and health issues.

A licensed psychologist in California, Dr. Backer holds a doctorate in psychology from the University of California at Los Angeles. He is a fellow of the American Psychological Association and a member of the Academy of Management. He is also a writer-producer of films and television programs, focusing on topics such as disability, mental illness, and aging. He counsels individual clients in the arts and entertainment fields, and has developed programs on creativity for many educational institutions. He has worked as a management consultant and educator in the arts and the entertainment industry for nearly 20 years.

Dr. Backer has been involved in several mass media campaigns that have had a component of high-risk youth in their target audiences, although none of the campaigns was focused exclusively on high-risk youth. He was a principal consultant and one of three PSA writers for the Facts for Life AIDS and drug abuse campaign on CBS Television. He also initiated (with Brian Dyak of the Entertainment Industries Council) the Carter Center Mental Illnesses and Entertainment Media Initiative, which is concerned with shaping public attitudes about treatment facilities, treatment professionals, and families of the severely mentally ill.

*   *   *

What are the most common reasons mass media campaigns do not achieve their hoped-for results, and what are the most common reasons some campaigns are relatively successful?

One of the most important factors affecting the success of a campaign is the availability of *resources* and, in particular, some amount of hard cash, in addition to contributions of labor and services. There are some campaign expenses that can't be "comped"—they have to be paid for directly.

Another factor is *leadership*. In many mass media campaigns, where large amounts of collaborative effort are required by various agencies, there often is no single person in charge of the overall campaign. Although a certain amount of sharing of power is essential in any collaborative effort, some person must have a vision of the campaign's direction, along with the leadership abilities and the authority to keep the campaign on track. For example, in the Facts for Life campaign, the person with the vision was Brian Dyak of the Entertainment Industries Council (EIC).

Campaigns often fail either because the aims and goals (the focus) of the campaign are not clearly defined or because the aims are too ambitious. When campaign aims are not defined and delimited, there is a tendency to try to keep all the contributors to the campaign happy, and the message content is watered down so much that it has no impact at all.

How could present health communication campaign models be improved to make them useful for planning, implementing, and evaluating mass media campaigns?

The available models of public communication campaigns are seldom utilized in planning a campaign, but are instead used only after a campaign is completed, to analyze its effects. The reason the models are not being used for planning is that they *lack applicability* to campaign design in real-world, practical situations. For example, the roles of financial, political, and social interaction factors, and the personalities and styles of the main players, are not taken into account in these models nearly as much as would be desirable.

Another problem is the *time constraints* of media campaigns. Campaign products have to be delivered to the media on a deadline. Existing models are too cumbersome to design campaigns in short periods of time. Hence the models are difficult to use as planning devices. The models could be made more useful by translating them into action-oriented guidelines, strategies, and standards. This might be done first by "retrofitting" models onto successful, completed campaigns and then drawing down from that a streamlined approach.

What roles can formative or summative evaluation play in the relative success of a health communication campaign?

Formative evaluation is critical to the success of a media campaign. In addition to helping with initial planning, formative evaluation is useful for improving a campaign while it is under way. Mass media campaigns are often unsuccessful because their designers have little idea of the real characteristics of the target audience. Methods are needed to generate warning signals if a recently introduced campaign is ineffective. In such cases, formative evaluation can be utilized to redesign the campaign. Media campaigns are often difficult to change in mid-course, because oftentimes reasons other than just to have an impact on a target audience govern how a campaign is run. For instance, politicians wish to get elected, or some influential person or group insists that the messages be put in a certain kind of way. These factors may determine how a campaign is run more than whether or not its basic operating strategy works.

Summative evaluation is important for advancing our knowledge of what worked and what didn't in media campaigns. Such evaluation is useful for determining whether a media campaign approach indeed had enough benefit that it should be used again. For example, the summative evaluation of the Stop the Madness campaign conducted by the EIC was instrumental in convincing CBS, the National Institute on Drug Abuse, and other agencies to collaborate in the Facts for Life campaign. Summative evaluation can measure how much airtime was donated and used, the awards won, and the number of people reached. With enough resources, it can also estimate actual behavior change, though this is difficult and expensive.

What are the unique characteristics and special difficulties of preventive health communication campaigns, especially those aimed at high-risk youth?

The most important difficulty with preventive health campaigns is the concept of "prevention" itself, as a change in present behavior reducing the possibility of negative consequences in the future. Western society traditionally has a poor understanding of the long-term consequences of present behavior, and does a poor job of communicating the notion of prevention. Children are seldom taught about conceptual foresight—the anticipation of consequences of current actions, and planning based on likely scenarios for an uncertain future. Youth are at an age where lots of experimenting is going on, where much rebelling is happening against authority figures, and a very strong perception of invulnerability is pervasive. Preventive campaign strategies that are effective with youth draw heavily upon the consequences that have immediate payoffs for them, for example, acceptance by peers or help in getting dates. It is sometimes difficult for campaign designers to accept this reality because they remain emotionally tied to the contents of their campaign messages and to *their* view of the world rather than that of their target audience.

How do factors such as age groupings, fear appeals, audience segmentation, and use of opinion leaders contribute to the design of mass media campaigns targeted to high-risk youth?

It is better to intervene at as early an age as is possible for effective prevention. In the case of substance abuse, the intervention should be before the age of experimentation starts. If values related to health behavior are communicated at an early age, it becomes easier to communicate prevention behavior in later years. Data about media preferences and life activities in the various subgroups of youth should be readily available, since many media campaigns have been conducted already with these audiences.

Unless fear appeals are done very cleverly, the evidence suggests that a negative reaction will be produced. The audience tends to discount the message or to behave counter to the message, or to simply deny the message. Punishment, fear, or negative reinforcement is not useful in teaching people new ideas. The exception is if the fear is simply used to get attention, or if it relates to highly valued and immediate outcomes, such as social rejection.

Segmentation of the audience is very important, especially for racial, ethnic, and minority groups. The nature of the content of a campaign (including the message) and the nature of the behavior that is to be changed differ for different people.

Identification of opinion leaders rests on finding ways of "getting into" the system. Opinion leaders who are identified initially can help identify others who can help, and the initial opinion leaders can work to get these others involved. One must make it clear to opinion leaders that they are going to be taken seriously and will not be exploited—a trustful relationship is essential for success.

A good example of incentives for creating grass-roots involvement is a campaign conducted by the Scott Newman Center in Los Angeles. The campaign involves an annual competition for the design of a television antidrug PSA for high school children, with the best entry actually being produced for airing, sometimes on national television. Such programs create real involvement and a sense of accomplishment in the target audience. Disincentives are not very useful because they involve fear and punishment-related effects.

The work of the Entertainment Industries Council with minority audience media, especially Spanish-language radio stations, is an example of the effective use of alternative communication channels. We have missed many opportunities for reaching target audiences through community-specific radio stations. Because of the glamour attached to advertisements on television networks and in large-circulation magazines, we have lost sight of the fact that radio is a very effective communication channel, especially for minority high-risk audiences. Other channels of communication for this audience might be comics and street-corner education groups.

The most effective mass-interpersonal communication relationship could involve some articulated tie-in between the mass media message and what happens at the local community level. For example, in the Just Say No campaign the message was in the mass media as well as in other channels, such as T-shirts and posters, and also was being disseminated through small group meetings of parents and children with teachers. This campaign illustrated how effective it can be to have a simple message repeated continuously, through different media.

Diversity of media used at different points in the lifetime of a campaign can be valuable. If radio PSAs, television PSAs, comic books, street-corner education groups, poster contests, song contests, and so on can be blended together in an effective and coordinated manner, the resulting campaign can be effective. Some channels can be used simultaneously, others in sequence—either to build impact or to stretch resources. Another advantage of multiple channels of communication is that the campaign attracts attention and creates a perception that the campaign is vigorous and is in fact reaching a large audience. That helps to get more people and organizations to collaborate in a campaign.

What is the most successful mass media campaign to change health behavior you have known, and why do you think it worked?

One of the most successful campaigns was the Stanford Heart Disease Prevention Program. The program had adequate resources, social scientists were closely involved in the project, the project was continued over a long period of time, and ensuring future replicability of the strategy was built into the design of the campaign. Several campaigns conducted by the Entertainment Industries Council have had success, such as Stop the Madness and a seat belt awareness campaign. Mostly this is because they have had continuity and because EIC has been willing to experiment with new media approaches and has enjoyed a solid working relationship with the commercial entertainment media at all levels.

What role should federal, state, or local governments play in media campaigns?

Many mass media campaigns have a partnership role with the government at some level. The main role that the government can play is that of a *catalyst* by providing start-up and out-of-pocket expense funding for a campaign, which other participants would not be willing to pay for. For example, the Facts for Life campaign would not have been so successful if the federal government had not provided the initial funding of $100,000. This funding was minuscule compared with the $8 million of free airtime donated by CBS Television. The start-up funding allowed the campaign designers to focus on campaign development, and not to worry about financing what the CBS network was not willing to pay for. The federal government can play an important role in underwriting drug prevention education in schools, to help promote the effects of mass media campaigns.

What organizations or organizational factors contribute to the success or failure of media campaigns?

Those who serve in a leadership role, conceptualizing media campaigns and bringing together the various elements of them, need to be knowledgeable about the campaign content area, mass media, and politics at various levels. This is not an easy task, and good campaign designers are not easy to find! Campaign designers must motivate decision makers in organizations they wish to involve in their campaigns. Such motivation must go beyond just being socially responsible, as individual self-interest is ultimately a more powerful motivator than social service. This can be seen, for instance, in the success of the Facts for Life campaign, where CBS Television had a chance to promote its fall programs and *also* serve a social cause.

EDWIN CHEN
Los Angeles Times

ABOUT THE INTERVIEWEE

Edwin Chen is a Science Writer in the Washington Bureau of the *Los Angeles Times*. He has also worked as Assistant Metro Editor, Metro Section, Legal Affairs Writer, and Staff Writer for that same publication, and free-lances for such publications as *The New York Times Magazine, The Atlantic, The Nation, The Progressive, People*, and the *Washington Post*. He is a contributing author to *Science of the (New York) Times* (Arno, 1981) and author of *PBB: An American Tragedy* (Prentice-Hall, 1979).

Mr. Chen has been the recipient of the Silver Gavel Award from the American Bar Association (1985), the Golden Medallion Award from the State Bar of California (1983 and 1984), and the United Press International Award of Merit (1977). He earned his B.A. in journalism from the University of South Carolina in 1970 and was a Nieman Fellow at Harvard University, 1984-1985.

*   *   *

In what campaigns have you been involved (including campaigns targeted to substance abuse and high-risk youth), and what role did you play?

The U.S. surgeon general might say that smoking is bad or eating fatty food is detrimental for health, and heart disease prevention might be featured in a campaign by a government agency. But the *L.A. Times* does not see itself involved as a partner with, or part of, such public education campaigns for health. The job of the *L.A. Times* is to cover the news. The newspaper might handle campaign press releases and promotional materials or report on the statements of different media campaign officials as long as such material is considered *newsworthy.* The newspaper does not see itself as conducting any kind of media campaign in health or in other areas.

Editorial decisions are made to do certain stories, projects, or a series about some specific issue. The paper might report information regarding this issue. For example, the paper might write news stories on how to lose weight or measures to reduce the likelihood of AIDS transmission, but it does not see itself as part of a campaign to combat AIDS or other health problems. The *Times* does inform readers who might be interested in losing weight or in taking precautions for safe sex. The newspaper also seeks to inform its readers about what the government and government officials, other agencies, and concerned people are doing or not doing in combating AIDS or other health issues. This perspective about media campaigns is important to an understanding of what a major newspaper like the *L.A. Times* will or will not do with respect to a mass media campaign.

What are the most common reasons mass media campaigns do not achieve their hoped-for results, and what are the most common reasons some campaigns are relatively successful?

A reason for success of any communication, as part of a campaign or otherwise, is how well a message gets across to the intended audience. A public communication campaign has many aspects, perhaps including advertising and direct appeals. One aspect involves getting the campaign message out through the news media, and to that extent the print news media *are* involved in campaigns. News certainly creates awareness and provides information, but it is difficult to quantify to what extent it contributes to attitude and behavior change. For example, in reporting the AIDS epidemic, the news media and especially the *L.A. Times* have written a lot about risk factors in the transmission of HIV. Surely some of these messages get through, and as a result some people will have refrained from unprotected sex or sharing needles or other high-risk activities. Campaign messages transmitted through news reports contribute to the general communication to certain target audiences that is going on in the environment of a campaign. Certainly these messages have played a role in combating the AIDS epidemic by raising health consciousness.

How do factors such as age groupings, fear appeals, audience segmentation, and use of opinion leaders contribute to the design of mass media campaigns targeted to high-risk youth?

The *L.A. Times* in its news stories tries not to scare its readers, but to present the facts as they are. Readers can then make a choice about certain health behaviors for themselves. The *L.A. Times* does not know how many of its readers are drug users or how many drug users use needles or how many indulge in unsafe sex practices. News is reported that appeals to the largest audience.

The newspaper does not segment its audience. People of different age groups and ethnic groups buy the newspaper for something they like in it—some for sports news, some for leisure information, and some for business news. There is something for everybody in the paper. The different parts of the newspaper are not necessarily targeted to different segments of the population, although they do represent specific interests.

What role should federal, state, or local governments play in media campaigns?

Leaders in strategic positions in government agencies or elsewhere, who have some standing and credibility, can get their message out relatively easier by appealing to the news media, through a press conference or press statements, or by issuing a white paper the news media can review and quote. It is not the job of the news media to motivate such leaders except to the extent that a person or an agency is not doing enough to correct a certain problem. A newspaper, through its editorial pages or through analytical news stories, may put pressure on certain agencies or individuals to act more responsibly in certain situations or in tackling certain health issues.

Multimedia communication campaigns have more effects than single-medium treatments. Television, because it reaches a larger population, may be more effective than newspapers in a mass media campaign, but the ideal campaign is one in which a number of media outlets are working synergistically.

The role of the government is to conduct public communication campaigns, and the role of the press is to convey news. Government campaigns are didactic in teaching style and convey a persuasive message, whereas the print news media try to enlighten people beyond just simply trying to tell them how to prevent or cure a problem. It is not the job of the press to work hand in hand with the government in conducting health campaigns. The job of the press is more of a "watchdog" over government representatives and agencies, to see that government is doing its job properly. With an issue like AIDS, many competing and conflicting interests and viewpoints may exist, many of which are contrary to official government policies. To be sure that these points of view are reported fairly, the press must maintain its independence.

The broadcast media are required under the federal government's Fairness Doctrine to provide free airtime for public service announcements. But the print media do not have such a role and are under no obligation to run such advertisements. I would not say to federal agencies, "Let's get together and figure out what we should write about a health issue." We do not want them to tell us what to do, just as they do not want us to tell them what to do.

What organizations and organizational factors contribute to the success or failure of media campaigns?

Campaign designers must keep certain realities in mind if they wish to collaborate effectively with news media organizations in a health campaign. For instance, there is no agreed-upon definition of *news value*, but one basic definition is, what is generally *new*. Reporters for the print news media do not want to write about some topic that is not new. That does not mean that stories about "old" issues are not written; a proper perspective presents some old news also. A newspaper will not write about information that is already known, but it may write about old issues from a new perspective.

PATRICK C. COLEMAN
Johns Hopkins University

ABOUT THE INTERVIEWEE

Patrick C. Coleman is Associate Director of Population Communication Services (PCS) in the School of Hygiene and Public Health at Johns Hopkins University, where he has pioneered using popular music to carry the family planning message to millions of young people and adults in Latin America, the Philippines, and West Africa. For example, in 1988 popular Latin American singers Tatiana and Johnny performed a smash hit, "Cuando Estemos Juntos" ("When We Are Together"), that spread the message of teenage sexual abstinence and contraception. Coleman has worked at all levels of campaign design, implementation, and operation.

Mr. Coleman is a former Peace Corps volunteer in El Salvador. He earned a master's degree in sociology from the University of Chicago. He is currently serving as the PCS Country Director in the Philippines.

* * *

What are the most common reasons mass media campaigns do not achieve their hoped-for results, and what are the most common reasons some campaigns are relatively successful?

There are often unrealistic expectations for a mass media health campaign. Also, there are often insufficient budget allocations for these projects. Professionals from different areas are not available to work together at the same time, which provides a further complication. For example, the successful Tatiana and Johnny project in Latin America cost $200,000, and involved professionals from many fields. A network of supplementary services is needed to tie into the mass media campaign to make it work at the community level. For example, halfway houses, youth centers, peer educators, sympathetic adults, counseling hot lines, and the like can be involved in a teenage pregnancy campaign.

How could present health communication campaign models be improved to make them useful for planning, implementing, and evaluating mass media campaigns?

The present communication models for campaigns generally work, although we need to know more about behavioral change and how it comes about. An important component not emphasized enough in the current models, though, is the degree of *message repetition* required in a successful campaign. Seldom can goals be achieved with only one campaign message. The advertising community does not think it can achieve brand shifts for a product within one day or with one message. They know it takes a long time, several months or years.

What roles can formative or summative evaluation play in the relative success of a health communication campaign?

Formative evaluation is absolutely imperative. "Behind-the-desk" perceptions are not useful—the evaluations must get out to the public being served the campaign. In the United States, campaigns do not utilize formative research to the same extent as the approach is used in Third World countries, with resulting deficits in campaign operations. Summative evaluation should not be looked upon as providing a "report card" (as is usually done), but as feedback for drawing lessons for future campaigns. All of the media campaigns mounted in Third World countries by Johns Hopkins University's Population Communication Services are evaluated in this way.

What are the unique characteristics and special difficulties of preventive health communication campaigns, especially those aimed at high-risk youth?

Youth can be reached only through a limited number of channels, so reaching them is difficult. The message must be simple, and, more important, the everyday language of youth has to be used, which again is limited by the channel used. Music dominates the lives of youth, and so it is one effective way of reaching them. Johns Hopkins University's Population Communication Services has used popular music to reach youth in the Philippines and throughout Latin America. In West Africa, we used a song, "Choices," to reach adults with a message about family responsibility.

How do factors such as age groupings, fear appeals, audience segmentation, and use of opinion leaders contribute to the design of mass media campaigns targeted to high-risk youth?

The age group of 10 to 13 years is an appropriate segment of youth to target in campaigns. Fear appeals are not useful, particularly with youth. Fear arouses negative emotions that linger on, and they can have a negative impact. Rational, positive emotional appeals are more useful. Fear may be effective mainly as an attention getter.

Audience segmentation into small, workable groups is necessary. It is wrong to treat youth as just one large, homogeneous group. We must take into account their ethnic origins and economic, religious, age, and gender differences.

To find opinion leaders, more research on role models needs to be conducted. However, youth talking to youth, without using older role models, is typically the best strategy. For example, a teenage rock star like Tatiana was very effective because youth identify with youth even though the individual may be from a different background. The evaluation study of the Tatiana and Johnny campaign in Latin America showed that their song led youth to discuss the topics of sexual abstinence and contraception more freely. A relatively young person who has passed through the same life experiences (such as a former drug addict) might be very effective as a role model in a drug abuse campaign.

Incentives/disincentives can take youth only to a certain point in behavior change, such as whether or not to participate in an activity. For example, giving a free T-shirt can induce youth to participate in an evaluation research interview, but we cannot expect such an incentive to stop them from having unsafe sex. Material incentives such as free food are better than monetary incentives. Disincentives, on the other hand, do not work well with youth in promoting attitude or behavior change.

Mass and interpersonal communication strategies are inseparable in a campaign. Mass media are required to provide information, and interpersonal communication methods are needed to promote actual behavior change. In addition to TV and radio, posters can be effective, especially in places where youth hang out.

A campaign media mix depends on the audience and on what segment of the target audience is to be reached. Television is the most powerful medium, but it is expensive and so requires a larger budget for the campaign. Radio can deliver more explicit messages without creating much controversy. For instance, the Catholic church in Mexico did not object to the Tatiana and Johnny song.

Print media generally are not very effective in media campaigns for youth. Newspapers may be good for informing outreach workers who work with these youth, but not their clients. Movie theaters in the United States are not used for "social commercials," as they are in Third World countries. These social commercials are short features shown before a movie; concerned with some health or social issue, done in an entertainment mode, they can be very effective.

What is the most successful mass media campaign to change health behavior you have known, and why do you think it worked?

The UNICEF immunization campaigns have been very successful. The reasons for their success include total support from key people (in government, health, media, religion, and so on) for the campaign and its objectives. The UNICEF campaigns have virtually no negative connotations, are not perceived as a threat to the family, are a discreet activity, and require only a one-day commitment. Thousands of people were mobilized to work in the campaigns.

What role should federal, state, or local governments play in media campaigns?

Government should play a larger role in mass media health campaigns, but with certain limitations. Usually this means serving in a financial capacity. Government agencies are concerned about the potential of political fallout from a campaign, and so government employees involved in campaigns tend to protect themselves and their jobs. Governments are reluctant to take risks. The federal government should invest more *money* in health campaigns, but media and health professionals must do the implementing.

What organizations and organizational factors contribute to the success or failure of media campaigns?

In any communication campaign, media support is needed, because there is never enough money to broadcast messages with adequate frequency. In addition, campaign support from the artistic community and from celebrities is helpful. University scholars have an evaluation research capability that can be utilized to the advantage of media campaigns. The organizations involved in implementing media campaigns must have a commitment, they must sense the problem that the campaign addresses, and such organizations must know what and how to speak to the target audience.

What methods would you suggest for financing media campaigns for health?

A combination of entertainment and education is a good strategy for financing media campaigns—delivering a health message in a commercial entertainment product, such as Tatiana and Johnny's song, which was highly successful financially. However, the success of this strategy depends on a high-quality, slick product. The focus should be on entertainment first (to generate money and exposure for the campaign message), and then on the message content itself.

Corporate sponsorship of campaign activities has not been explored enough. The corporate community should be invited to make financial contributions, as well as to provide materials to the campaign. Such sponsorship does not lower the credibility of the health message. On the contrary, corporate sponsorship may well legitimate the campaign activity in the eyes of politicians, who then think that it is not just one small organization such as an advocacy group trying to promote a given health message. In campaigns where this corporate sponsorship strategy has been utilized, there has been little negative feedback from young people or their parents regarding the sponsorship. The key point is to have a good-quality product. For instance, the Tatiana and Johnny song, "Cuando Estemos Juntos" ("When We Are Together"), was immensely popular in Mexico and Latin America. The evaluation study showed that the song was played an average of 15 times per day for three months by the typical radio station in Mexico. Such repeated exposure is one reason for its effectiveness in teaching teenagers about sexual abstinence and contraception.

LARRY DEUTCHMAN
Entertainment Industries Council

ABOUT THE INTERVIEWEE

Larry Deutchman is Director of Program Development and Creative Affairs for the nonprofit Entertainment Industries Council. His responsibilities include development of new projects; overseeing ongoing programs; generating merchandising, marketing, and promotional opportunities; and creative and production involvement in EIC media campaigns, videos, and broadcast and cable television specials and series.

Since 1986, he has been instrumental in the growth of EIC's production capabilities, having written and executive produced *Buckle Up*, an educational film that won a number of international awards, including the CINE Golden Eagle (the nontheatrical equivalent of an Oscar). His public service campaigns have earned international broadcasting awards, including the Mobius Broadcasting Award, three Markie Awards, and four Buccaneer Awards. Deutchman has served as writer, director, producer, executive producer, or development executive on several productions, including *That's a Wrap, Mythbusters, Stop the Madness,* the National Red Ribbon Campaign, and a Texas Prevention Partnership video.

Mr. Deutchman is currently in production on EIC's latest promotional video and educational film for the Texas Prevention Partnership (a major state-sponsored substance abuse prevention effort conducted by EIC) on the devastating effects of inhalant abuse. He has also developed creative print materials such as advertisements, posters, press kits, and school curricula for EIC. He has consulted with the entertainment industry creative community on depiction of public service issues in television and motion picture production, as well as in comic books and newspaper comic strips.

Prior to his employment at EIC, Deutchman served as Director of Public Relations for the National Safety Council, where he founded the Entertainment Industry Committee on Safety Belts. He has also served two terms on the board of directors of the Public Interest Radio and Television Educational Society, and is a member of the Entertainment Industry Coalition on AIDS and of the Entertainment Industry Workplace AIDS Committee.

*   *   *

What are the most common reasons mass media campaigns do not achieve their hoped-for results, and what are the most common reasons some campaigns are relatively successful?

One of the reasons many media campaigns do not achieve good results is because they lack follow-through on a consistent basis to make sure that campaign activities are implemented properly. Another reason is unrealistic expectations about what mass media alone can actually accomplish; if a program's goals are set only by what the mass media component can do, the program is compromised from the start. A third reason is bad targeting. Campaign designers often are so concerned about trying to get across a generic message through the "safest" (that is, least controversial) means that the message gets diluted in trying to reach a mass market. Also, the people who conduct health campaigns often lack sufficient knowledge of how the mass media industry works. For example, campaign designers may complete production of their

PSAs only two or three days before their campaign's "awareness week." Then they hope that the PSAs will be broadcast during that week, when the usual lead time for submission of PSAs to a television or radio station in advance of their airing is at least four to six weeks.

How could present health communication campaign models be improved to make them useful for planning, implementing, and evaluating mass media campaigns?

Campaign models are based on theory; successful campaigns include theory, but also a lot of practical advance legwork and thorough planning. The contacts and the channels should be worked out, from the production as well as the distribution side, right from the start. Also, it should be made clear that the campaign designers are "partners," and not adversaries of the community or in the sphere of influence in which the campaign is conducted. A campaign should never be launched to attack the way in which something is being done in the local community.

Successful campaigns to change media depiction of an issue involve the entertainment/communication industry as partners, not as adversaries. A campaign should try to work from "inside" rather than impose itself from "outside." A mass media campaign should utilize a peer-to-peer approach with insiders working from a positive standpoint, rather than outsiders working from a negative standpoint.

What roles can formative or summative evaluation play in the relative success of a health communication campaign?

Behavior change is not a product of one single element in a mass media health campaign. Behavior change results from multiple activities: legislation, community activities, interaction with other agencies, and media effects. So it is difficult to pinpoint which cause is influencing a particular campaign effect. Moreover, the kinds of *effects* a campaign may have are complex. Therefore, campaign evaluation strategies cannot use the same approaches that work when measuring a product's purchase as the result of advertising.

What are the unique characteristics and special difficulties of preventive health communication campaigns, especially those aimed at high-risk youth?

One major challenge in breaking through cultural or other barriers to reaching a particular target group is that the target group has to be properly researched to find out how the messages are getting across and are being modified. A sociological and behavioral approach must be taken. For example, we should look at a target subgroup's purchasing trends, what the priorities are in their lives, and the approaches that commercial advertisers are taking with that particular group. If advertisers can make high-risk youth (especially those in the lower socioeconomic strata) spend money, other behavior changes can be accomplished also.

How do factors such as age groupings, fear appeals, audience segmentation, and use of opinion leaders contribute to the design of mass media campaigns targeted to high-risk youth?

Teenage to early 20s is the age range where the maximum risks to good health are initially taken. It is important to reach this high-risk audience early, but it is more helpful to reach them a little later, when there is more likely to be some logic and experience base to build on, compared with very young audiences. With a slightly older audience, more sophisticated messages can be used.

We do not take enough risks in the way we approach public service advertising. We have to make public service communications flashy, and use life-style advertising approaches. We cannot motivate youth with nontangible benefits. We have to hit them through the kinds of motivations they respond to, as seen in their buying habits. We approach public service advertisements moralistically (by depicting good and bad behaviors) when we are competing against beer and tobacco advertising that depicts life-style commercials showing it is "fun and wonderful to drink." We portray that "it is more responsible not to drink." We should create an image that *"it is fun and wonderful not to drink."* This is the best way to reach youth, especially high-risk youth. Most people know about the dangers of risky behaviors, but they go ahead and do risky things anyway because they want the immediate benefits and instant gratification. We have to approach public service ads from an instant gratification viewpoint! We have to portray healthy life-styles as glamorous, and "stretch the imagination" of the teenage audience, as paid advertising does when selling commercial products.

For some situations fear appeals are effective, but often they may cause too much anxiety to be successful. For most youth, creating fear is not helpful. Life-style depiction is the bottom line. Youth believe they are indestructible and immortal. Peer pressure is dominant in their decisions. Fear might have an effect on teenage audiences from the standpoint of tangible effects such as disfigurement or becoming physically handicapped, but not death. With youth we must use an emotional approach, and offer something that is tangible that they can relate to.

Audience segmentation used to seem unimportant, but too often we are busy trying to "convert the converted." Also, large populations are missed in many campaigns. Generic messages do not have any impact on the subgroups most in need of the information. We have to follow the example of paid advertising, which utilizes quite specific segmentation. We have to take different approaches, use different media, different role models, for different subgroups; create an approach that each "subaudience" can relate to. The environment as well as the culture determine what the activities and behaviors of the target audience are. It will be more helpful if we start segmenting by *behavior*, by the characteristics of the target audience, and by what *life-style* the target audience identifies with. For example, the audience segment that gears its activities around baseball could be approached by a life-style depiction that relates to baseball.

For different audience segments, different role models are effective. For example, for Hispanic populations, entertainment role models are effective; for the African-American population, sports celebrities tend to have more influence. We can find leaders in the school system, law enforcement, and other groups that have traditionally been involved in health issues. An underused resource are individuals in the media (newscasters, public affairs show hosts, and so on) who are positively inclined toward an issue and who can build public opinion within their communities.

The best incentive is to show the target youth the rewards of a nonabuse life-style. Alternative activities should be fun. Disincentives can be provided by "humanizing" (not judging) the people in the community who have suffered undesirable consequences from their risky behavior.

Television is an effective channel for public service announcements, and for depiction and explanation of health behavior issues in entertainment programming. Posters, if graphically appealing, contemporary, and visually exciting, may have some impact. Young people listen to a lot of radio, and this is an underutilized medium for health campaigns. But we have to start developing campaigns by finding out *how* the target youth spend their time, and then discover the appropriate communication channels to reach them. Another way of reaching youth is through "events," such as contests in local communities.

Mass and interpersonal communication strategies should be coordinated in local communities. In one substance abuse prevention campaign, EIC handled the media component and local voluntary organizations did the outreach component, but all aspects were carefully coordinated so that they worked together. However, coordination cannot be effective if a commitment from the media for cooperation and airplay is not obtained first.

What is the most successful mass media campaign to change health behavior you have known, and why do you think it worked?

From a short-term standpoint, the We Are the World campaign (for Ethiopian drought and hunger relief in 1985) generated a lot of fallout because important people got together to perform, with a common theme in mind. Mothers Against Drunk Driving (MADD) has created an atmosphere in which it has become unacceptable to drink and drive. This group's genuine sense of outrage made a difference. They made themselves heard and they brought the "outrage approach" to the news media, to talk shows, and to community rallies and activities. But the bottom line is that none of MADD's accomplishments could have been achieved without the media. The best way to reinforce a message is through depiction of responsible behavior on entertainment programming, so that the normal nature of the desired behavior is maintained.

What role should federal, state, or local governments play in media campaigns?

The federal government needs to take a leadership role in health campaigns by being willing to take risks in funding approaches to public service advertising. The government is doing a good job of encouraging community leaders to get involved in media campaigns, and of fostering partnerships with the private sector. The government should mobilize people behind an issue and then allow the motivated people to do the bulk of the work.

What organizations and organizational factors contribute to the success or failure of media campaigns?

It is not good to have the commitment only of the head of an organization. People at all levels in the organization have to be interested enough to work on a mass media health campaign, or it will be less effective. A partnership must be worked out among the various organizations at various levels. The Ad Council has been successful in getting its projects accepted by the television networks because it represents the buyer clout of the advertising agencies.

What methods would you suggest for financing media campaigns for health?

We have to get past the idea of foundations and corporate giving, as they do not have enough money to go around. We must solicit from a promotional standpoint from the private sector. We have to learn how to tie in programs with the products that companies sell, and learn to tie in with companies' public relations, advertising, and promotional budgets. These vehicles for financing mass media health campaigns have been little used thus far.

BRIAN DYAK
Entertainment Industries Council

ABOUT THE INTERVIEWEE

Brian Dyak is President and cofounder of the nonprofit Entertainment Industries Council. He is a nationally known policy development strategist and cause-oriented marketing specialist. He is also a producer of cause-oriented videos and significant, nationally recognized radio and television public service campaigns. He provides services regularly to various federal agencies such as the National Institute on Drug Abuse; the U.S. Department of Education; the Alcohol, Drug Abuse and Mental Health Administration; the Office for Substance Abuse Prevention; and the National Highway Traffic Safety Administration. He has been a consultant to the White House Conference for a Drug Free America, and has testified before numerous congressional committees on such issues as drug abuse prevention, alcohol beverage advertising standards, runaway and homeless youth, and youth employment policy. He has been featured on *ABC World News Tonight With Peter Jennings, NBC Nightly News With Tom Brokaw*, and numerous CNN news specials.

Mr. Dyak has been active as a consultant to the Rosalynn Carter Mental Health Symposium over the last three years, facilitating development of the Carter Center Mental Illnesses and Entertainment Media Initiative. He has led efforts within the entertainment industry to involve the creative community in depictions of drug abuse, AIDS, seat belt awareness, and mental illness. He has been the executive producer for several campaigns, such as the That's a Wrap seat belt use awareness campaign, the Stop Shooting Up AIDS campaign, the Drug-Free America campaign, Facts for Life, and the Stop the Madness antidrug campaign. Many of these campaigns were targeted to high-risk youth.

*　　*　　*

What are the most common reasons mass media campaigns do not achieve their hoped-for results, and what are the most common reasons some campaigns are relatively successful?

One reason campaigns are not successful is that the messages are inappropriate and culturally insensitive to the target audience. Many times the media mix in a campaign is not correct for the desired target audience—the channels available for use are not the ones that capture the target audience. Campaigns generally suffer from a lack of believability, and they tend to lack elements that make them competitive with commercial advertising and commercial public relations campaigns.

When there is proper segmentation of the audience, along with appropriate targeting of messages and the adequate use of delivery intermediaries, the mass media campaign triggers interpersonal communications and involves others (family members, friends, etc.) in the behavior change process. This involvement of ongoing interpersonal communication is critical for the success of media campaigns.

How could present health communication campaign models be improved to make them useful for planning, implementing, and evaluating mass media campaigns?

The models and the works of campaign researchers such as Charles Atkin, Everett Rogers, and Brian Flay have all provided strong campaign planning models for practitioners. However, some practical changes would make the models more helpful. For instance, it would help greatly to develop technical assistance programs for practitioners (campaign designers) so they could better apply the concepts suggested by these models. Also, consultant pools of experts proficient in campaign materials design would provide much of benefit to campaign designers.

What roles can formative or summative evaluation play in the relative success of a health communication campaign?

Formative evaluation is helpful to guide audience segmentation for knowledge, attitudes, and behavior change related to the campaign issue. Formative research can also help determine the potential reach of the campaign and which communication channels to use (e.g., traditional or alternative media). Formative research can help plan promotional strategies for the campaign or for the campaign products.

What are the unique characteristics and special difficulties of preventive health communication campaigns, especially those aimed at high-risk youth?

High-risk youth are difficult to reach due to their multiple risk behaviors and their resistance to media messages in many formats. A group to target would be teenagers who have already experienced health problems, and thus might be more likely to engage with health messages.

How do factors such as age groupings, fear appeals, audience segmentation, and use of opinion leaders contribute to the design of mass media campaigns targeted to high-risk youth?

Fear appeals are generally not effective, although they may grab attention and enhance awareness of the basic campaign issues.

Interpersonal, one-to-one communication channels are the most effective for changing attitudes. Such channels are particularly effective for social norm setting, so that people come to believe that the behavior promoted by the campaign is the norm. Examples of effective mass-interpersonal communication combinations are the responses to television shows, radio call-in shows, direct mail, and direct-response television advertising.

Existing combinations of media should be tried in a campaign, and new combinations formulated. Campaigns should target messages so that they show up in the home, in schools, and in the community at large, as opposed to reaching only the target audience in relative isolation, or solely through institutional settings.

What role should federal, state, or local governments play in media campaigns?

Federal, state, and local governments should focus on involving various channels of communication in health campaigns, and be open to testing various messages. Most important, government should provide a leadership role in mounting media campaigns and encouraging public-private partnerships.

What organizations or organizational factors contribute to the success or failure of media campaigns?

Incentives can be used creatively to motivate various types of organizations to contribute to a mass media health campaign: awarding special recognition, promotion of products through advertising tie-ins, and publicity benefits. Some perceived *disincentives* of association with a campaign to be overcome include thinking that corporate or personal (i.e., top management) image will suffer from the organization's participation, or that association with the campaign will be expensive. These issues have to be faced head-on in developing a campaign partnership.

The organizations involved in a media campaign sometimes lack the needed talent to fulfill their commitments—or they are loath to commit top talent to a voluntary project. Many campaigns are poorly planned, and poor use is made of the limited resources available for conducting a campaign.

What methods would you suggest for financing media campaigns for health?

Methods for raising financing for media campaigns include lotteries; multiple pro bono relationships and media collaborations, especially at the local level; tax-deduction incentives; and special government bonds. These should all be explored by campaign designers, though some of them would involve special legislative action before they could be used. But campaign designers of the future will need to think about such creative alternatives, since traditional sources of funding are likely to remain tight.

FERN FIELD
Brookfield Productions

ABOUT THE INTERVIEWEE

Fern Field is a writer-producer-director of commercial television programs whose works include a number of television movies and "after-school specials" for network television. She also has produced short motivational films designed to change people's attitudes toward physical and mental disabilities. In 1978, Field coproduced and directed her first featurette while on hiatus from Norman Lear's *Maude* television series. The film, titled *A Different Approach*, was a comedy-musical designed to encourage employment of people with disabilities; it won 20 prestigious national and international awards, including an Oscar nomination and the IFPA Best Directing Award. Shortly thereafter, Field directed four short films, *Science, Excellence, Careers,* and *Communications,* for Disney's Epcot Educational Media. In 1985 she produced and directed a half-hour documentary for the California Department of Mental Health titled *Just the Way You Are*, which has received a number of awards, including the New York International Film and Television Award.

Ms. Field has supervised productions in the United States, Canada, and Europe, with budgets ranging up to $15 million. She is a member of the Directors Guild of America, Writers Guild of America, Academy of Motion Picture Arts & Sciences, Academy of Television Arts & Sciences, and the Caucus for Producers, Writers & Directors. She has served on the board of Women in Film, and was President of that organization in 1987. In 1982, she received the Distinguished Service Award from President Reagan for her work with the disabled.

*   *   *

What are the most common reasons mass media campaigns do not achieve their hoped-for results, and what are the most common reasons some campaigns are relatively successful?

It is not clear whether or not motivational films or videos used in mass media campaigns achieve their hoped-for results. No single film or PSA produces direct behavior change. Instead, the contribution of a number of elements creates change in people's attitudes, and these have to be very carefully coordinated or the impact will be minimal. It is also very difficult to predict what effect a single media element will have.

What are the unique characteristics and special difficulties of preventive health communication campaigns, especially those aimed at high-risk youth?

Our campaign approaches do not address the real, underlying reasons why people are on drugs. Youths use drugs to get high because they live in a terrible world. When a youth sees the person next door making $500 a day selling crack, it is impossible to appeal to him or her about work that involves earning a minimum wage. We can make endless films and other messages, but we are not going to achieve behavior change, because we have not brought about change in the situations that youths find themselves in. People in high-risk situations have very good reasons not to participate in the world that *we* give them. Campaigns have to respond to these realities in some fashion.

How do factors such as age groupings, fear appeals, audience segmentation, and use of opinion leaders contribute to the design of mass media campaigns targeted to high-risk youth?

Many films for changing attitudes toward physical disabilities were successful because they allowed viewers to overcome their guilt and discomfort toward the issue. Society tends to look at a physical disability as a tragedy, and not to see the positive aspects of the physically disabled person. These films remove guilt by allowing viewers to look at a disabled person as a human being, and not focus just on his or her disabilities. No formal theory or research was utilized in making these films, but their format seems to fit with a lot of what seems to be coming out of mass communications theory.

The target audience also was studied informally to define the purpose of the films, whether they would spark conversation, and so forth. Evaluation of these films was done at the screenings. Before and after exposure, questionnaires were administered to audience members to determine whether their perceptions had changed as a result of watching the film. In the production of a film to combat illiteracy, although there was close collaboration with professional literacy experts, it is not certain that a more effective product was produced than would have been without this collaboration.

It is necessary to find out what the target audience is truly afraid of, and then to find specific ways to approach that fear in campaign messages. The general fear appeal that a certain behavior is not good for health is not very effective.

When Henry Winkler of *Happy Days* took out a library card, the next day U.S. libraries got thousands of requests for library cards. We have to look for media messages that groups of people are really susceptible to, as Henry Winkler's behavior seemed to have an impact on American teenagers.

Incentives of any particular type do not work with everyone. Their effectiveness depends on particular audiences and what their needs are—real and perceived. Providing real economic incentives that significantly alter the lives of high-risk people, such as offering an alternative to the drug money going into many minority communities, could be helpful in effecting behavior change. But this involves action far beyond media campaigns themselves.

Television is an effective channel, as it reaches almost everyone in all social strata. Radio may not be as effective as television, as the formats of message presentation are not so versatile. It would be helpful to know more about the profile of drug abusers as audience for radio, in order to improve the effectiveness of radio messages.

A campaign that comes bottom-up, from peer groups and the communities of high-risk youth, might be most effective. A campaign should not be constructed on the basis of an order from higher authority, or presented as an interference in the lives of those in the target audience of high-risk youth.

What is the most successful mass media campaign to change health behavior you have known, and why do you think it worked?

It is difficult to pinpoint a single most successful campaign. The American Heart Association campaigns are outstanding; so are several of the antismoking campaigns. The declining number of smokers is due to a combination of factors happening at the same time—a lot of messages at the same time through various channels, and generally changing social values plus more and more medical evidence.

What organizations and organizational factors contribute to the success or failure of media campaigns?

The help of the television networks and the Ad Council is crucial in most national media campaigns. These groups have the resources of airtime and creative talent to donate, resources so expensive no campaign can afford to buy them. Advocacy groups can counter the influence of the tobacco or the liquor lobby, and thus facilitate the implementation of campaigns on issues where economic interests are great.

What methods would you suggest for financing media campaigns for health?

Government agencies have lots of red tape and bureaucracy, but often provide some basic finances for media campaigns. Thus campaign designers need to continue looking to these audiences for support of their campaigns.

JUAN M. FLAVIER
International Institute of Rural Reconstruction, Philippines

ABOUT THE INTERVIEWEE

Juan M. Flavier is President of the Institute of Rural Reconstruction in the Philippines. He is particularly noted for his use of agricultural and rural analogies in diffusion of family planning methods to Filipino villagers. For instance, Dr. Flavier shows villagers the basic similarity between oral contraceptive pills and ipil-ipil seeds, which have a contraceptive effect on laying hens. Dr. Flavier earned his medical degree in the Philippines, and his master's degree in public health from Johns Hopkins University.

Dr. Flavier has had advisory, planning, and implementation experience in the family planning and population communication fields in the Philippines. Many of his mass media health campaigns have been targeted to rural youth in his country.

*   *   *

What are the most common reasons mass media campaigns do not achieve their hoped-for results, and what are the most common reasons some campaigns are relatively successful?

The language used in health media campaigns often is not appropriate for the target audience. This problem is especially apparent when scientific and technical words are utilized in a local language. The language is not culturally correct and does not fit in the targeted social context. The audience fails to identify with it and thus it has little impact. Also the message is often not repeated enough times to have the maximum desired effect.

How could present health communication campaign models be improved to make them useful for planning, implementing, and evaluating mass media campaigns?

Mass media are effective mainly for creating awareness, so media messages have to be followed up with interpersonal communication activities of various sorts. Therefore, the education of local leaders in the community is very important. Adolescents are generally fun-loving, so campaign messages should be entertaining. Also, the messages should start with something familiar to the target audience, and then build on the familiar to get new concepts across. For example, messages about family planning in rural areas can convey these ideas through the metaphor of agriculture.

The campaign should be related to some real event that has happened in the lives of the target audience. For example, if there has been a death due to cholera in the community, a campaign for building toilets or immunization should be related to this event, rather than to some more remote argument about "improving health." The localization of campaigns is important to their success, and even large-scale campaigns can be locally customized in certain ways with enough ingenuity and effort.

What roles can formative or summative evaluation play in the relative success of a health communication campaign?

Summative evaluation methodology is complex and often scares campaign people, so the concepts should be simplified and the terminology of evaluation should be changed. Summative evaluation, to be genuinely effective from a practical viewpoint, has to be participatory, involving the target audience and the fieldworkers, and flexible and nonexact (exactness serves little purpose) in its methodology.

Formative evaluation is important to guide the development of a campaign. It should be simple, participatory, nonthreatening, and presented appropriately to the target audience in order to get good results.

How do factors such as age groupings, fear appeals, audience segmentation, and use of opinion leaders contribute to the design of mass media campaigns targeted to high-risk youth?

Most drug problems occur in the transition from junior high school to senior high school, which involves the age group 12 to 15. Communication channels for reaching dropouts are few, and media campaigns for reaching these populations need to be explored.

Fear appeals are not very useful with youth, as such appeals tend unfortunately to create a "dare" reaction contradictory to the intended purpose. Campaign designers need to be very careful in looking for such dare reactions in testing their messages. Fear of father, fear of nonacceptance by family, fear of ridicule, and other basically social interpersonal fears may be more effective for dealing with young people.

Audience segmentation is especially important because health campaign resources are scarce. To motivate community leaders involved in campaigns, campaign designers should give them recognition, training, and responsibility for solving the problem that the campaign addresses.

Incentives have to be carefully thought out, or else they can backfire. Monetary incentives are usually not credible. Furthermore, most incentives should not be used repeatedly over time, as they lose their value and meaning. For example, certificates presented to honor campaign participants may be motivating the first year, but in a second year such certificates lose importance for most of the recipients.

What role should federal, state, or local governments play in media campaigns?

Government involvement generally should come during a later stage in a communication campaign. First, nongovernment organizations (NGOs) should implement the campaign on a small scale, and the campaign designers can learn from these experiences. The mistakes committed remain small. Later, the small success can be replicated into a big success. Government and NGOs have to work together. NGOs have the resources to undertake experimental pilot campaigns, but only a national government can implement a media campaign on a large scale.

What organizations and organizational factors contribute to the success or failure of media campaigns?

Medical doctors managing media campaigns suffer from their lack of training in dealing with people other than on a one-on-one basis. They find it difficult to think on a mass scale. Medical doctors also are not usually trained to delegate, they have less belief in the effectiveness of mass communication, and they usually do not allocate adequate resources for training campaign personnel.

Participation of the audience for a campaign in designing it is important. The targeted "subsubsegment" of a particular audience is a world in itself, and so the nearness of campaign workers to the audience and their values and life experiences is important. Some topics—abuse, family planning—are very sensitive and inherently fear provoking, so people surrounding the individual have to be mobilized in order for any effect to occur. Mass communication can create awareness, but only interpersonal communication can move an individual to action. Two types of people are usually close to youth: friends and confidants. A friend is usually from the adolescent's own peer group, while a confidant may be someone older, perhaps a close relative. Campaigns targeted to these audiences have good chances for success.

BRIAN FLAY
University of Illinois

ABOUT THE INTERVIEWEE

Brian Flay received his doctorate in social psychology from Waikato University in New Zealand in 1976. After receiving his postdoctoral training at Northwestern University under a Fulbright/Hays Fellowship, he conducted research on smoking prevention at the University of Waterloo in Ontario, Canada. He continued work on smoking prevention, and developed studies in the areas of drug prevention and the use of mass media for smoking cessation at the University of Southern California. Since 1987, Dr. Flay has directed the Prevention Research Center in the School of Public Health, University of Illinois at Chicago, where he continues his research in the above areas, as well as in AIDS prevention.

Dr. Flay serves on the editorial boards of *Health Education Research: Theory and Practice* and the *International Journal of the Addictions*.

He also serves on a number of advisory boards, committees, and expert panels for such organizations as the Office for Substance Abuse Prevention, the National Academy of Sciences, the American Medical Association, and the Chicago Lung Association.

*   *   *

What are the most common reasons mass media campaigns do not achieve their hoped-for results, and what are the most common reasons some campaigns are relatively successful?

Campaigns are often unsuccessful because they do not reach their intended target audiences, the message content is not theoretically based and so it is not convincing, the content is not designed in such a way as to change behavior, the messages do not get people involved (by getting them to pay attention, to talk to other people, or to take action as a result of the message), and the messages are not repeated with enough frequency over time. Successful campaigns have to deal with each of these challenges.

How could present health communication campaign models be improved to make them useful for planning, implementing, and evaluating mass media campaigns?

No one theory and no one model is totally adequate for designing public communication campaigns. Even the models that strive to integrate different models or approaches do not seem adequate at the present time, and much work is needed by campaign scholars to improve them.

What roles can formative or summative evaluation play in the relative success of a health communication campaign?

Formative evaluation should play a much more important role than it has played in most media campaigns. Formative evaluation can help to overcome some basic problems of quality of message content, and it can generally lead to more effective campaigns. Summative evaluation informs us of the effects of a campaign in the real world, and thus feeds into the knowledge base for future campaigns. Both formative and summative evaluation are underused in campaigns. People think about evaluation only as summative evaluation, when they think about it at all.

How do factors such as age groupings, fear appeals, audience segmentation, and use of opinion leaders contribute to the design of mass media campaigns targeted to high-risk youth?

Mass media campaigns for alcohol and other drug prevention can be designed for many age groups. Television can be useful for younger children, such as 8- to 12-year-olds, by showing them the negative social effects or critical peer pressure against tobacco use, and also by showing how to resist peer pressure for tobacco use. For teenagers, campaigns should use radio much more than they currently do. Little research has been done on what motivates kids to listen to certain media messages offered by campaigns, much less how they respond to them.

Fear appeals can be motivational and they can be highly effective. Their negative effects have been overrated. Fear appeals put a little twist on the message. An information approach would say that if you smoke you can get cancer. A fear appeal approach would present the same information with emotional appeals in a scary way. With fear appeals, we must make sure that the message provides ways of *resolving* the fear, or ways of *acting* on motivation that may have been created. Otherwise the fear message does not lead to the desired result, and may even have undesirable side effects.

Who adolescents define as a peer or an opinion leader is related to their friendship and group choices, which are related in turn to their relationships with their parents and their families. A kid coming from a family in which there is violence has a greater chance of identifying him- or herself with deviants or gang leaders than a kid who comes from a family where there is effective communication between parents and youth.

We have a very limited knowledge base about what incentives and disincentives are effective with youth. Main concerns of teenagers are often the desire for independence and the need to grow up into adult roles. If a campaign can provide a way of addressing these concerns, and at the same time provide an alternative to drugs, that campaign can be effective. Kids want to feel that they are becoming like adults and "making it" in the social world.

We can approach teenagers effectively through music—for instance, MTV and other music programs on both radio and TV. There are some important cultural differences: In many cases, white kids use television for entertainment, while black kids use television for escape. This may mean that black kids pay more attention to advertising than do white kids. We should direct messages to parents on nighttime television or radio, suggesting they talk to their kids about drug abuse.

What role should federal, state, or local governments play in media campaigns?

Public service announcements are usually a waste of resources unless they are aired at the proper times to reach their desired target audiences. To make this happen, government agencies should finance the buying of appropriate time slots for paid public service advertising (as determined by audience research). Government agencies also can serve as role models by insisting on formative research to develop effective campaigns and summative evaluations to understand their effects.

What organizations and organizational factors contribute to the success or failure of media campaigns?

A major organizational factor bearing on the success of mass media campaigns is who *controls the content* of the campaign messages. Moreover, it is difficult for the organization that develops the material also to have control over decisions on the airing of the messages. So different organizations hold bits and pieces of control over the campaign's conduct. In the ideal situation, a single authority should have total control over the complete campaign.

JUNE FLORA
Stanford University

ABOUT THE INTERVIEWEE

June Flora received her B.A. in psychology from Bridgewater College in 1971; she earned her M.A. and Ph.D. degrees in educational psychology from Arizona State University in 1974 and 1975, respectively. Following her graduate work, she served a clinical psychology internship at the University of Washington Medical School, then became a member of the Department of Educational Psychology faculty at the University of Utah from 1976 to 1979. In 1979 she was appointed a Postdoctoral Fellow in Cardiovascular Epidemiology and Preventive

Medicine at Stanford University's School of Medicine. Immediately following this, she became Director of Community Organization and then of the Education Program for the Stanford Heart Disease Prevention Program. Since 1986, she has been an Assistant Professor of Communication and an Associate Director of the Stanford Center for Research in Disease Prevention at Stanford.

Dr. Flora has authored or coauthored more than 30 peer-reviewed articles, monographs, and book chapters dealing with both theoretical and applied issues in communication campaigns designed for social changes, in health message effectiveness, and in health communication.

The campaign in which Dr. Flora has been most involved is the Stanford Heart Disease Prevention Program. Although this program was not directly targeted to youth, it had an active youth component aimed at changing adolescent dietary and smoking behavior.

* * *

What are the most common reasons mass media campaigns do not achieve their hoped-for results, and what are the most common reasons some campaigns are relatively successful?

Two sets of issues explain the relative success or failure of media campaigns: (1) empirical and theoretical reasons, and (2) practical and implementation-oriented reasons. Most media campaigns are not theory driven. Campaign activities are not well specified or ordered sequentially. The campaign is not targeted to specific audiences or based on an understanding of the audience. High-risk youth audiences are targeted by campaigns in schools, where few truly high-risk youth are present. So we do not reach the intended youth audience with the intended message. Sometimes we reach them with messages that are not of any interest to them, and so no impact occurs.

Some campaigns are successful because they have a theoretical basis, are systematic and well evaluated, and have messages appropriate to their desired behavior outcomes. The potential for campaign success is increased by using *skills-based message content*, which helps adolescents develop skills to manage high-risk situations.

What roles can formative or summative evaluation play in the relative success of a health communication campaign?

Formative and summative evaluation are critical, in both the pre-production and the production stages of audience segmentation, in message design, and in message testing for media campaigns. Evaluation activities relate to both the theoretical and practical aspects of campaign design.

What are the unique characteristics and special difficulties of preventive health communication campaigns, especially those aimed at high-risk youth?

The most critical difficulty faced by prevention campaigns aimed at youth is that we are asking young people to change their behavior relative to long-term goals, such as reducing morbidity and mortality and improving the quality of life. Adolescents cannot usually perceive the benefits of long-term outcomes. Short-term positive outcomes may not be as attractive as is the unhealthy behavior. So the goal of a campaign designer should be to promote the most appealing short-term outcomes for the behavior he or she is promoting.

High-risk youth may be engaged in a cluster of high-risk behaviors: They may drink alcohol, do drugs, be sexually active, have less developed support systems, be less achievement oriented, do less well in school, and be disenfranchised from other agencies that might be able to help them. So we are talking about a composite of behaviors that must be changed to make a significant difference in risk behavior, even in one particular area. It is difficult to imagine that one set of campaign messages could change the overall dimensions of a generally high-risk life-style, and good campaigns acknowledge this.

How do factors such as age groupings, fear appeals, audience segmentation, and use of opinion leaders contribute to the design of mass media campaigns targeted to high-risk youth?

From a long-term prevention perspective, the age group to target is younger children. We need to begin building perceptions about healthy behavior at a very young age. In later years, youth will have more arguments in store to use against undesirable health behaviors, and more understanding of the perceived benefits of desirable health behaviors. Another ideal time to intervene is just prior to young people's first encountering the situations in which they are exposed to the possibility of the undesirable behavior.

One should be quite specific with fear appeals. For example, fear that you may lose your boyfriend or girlfriend because of bad breath due to smoking will probably be a more powerful fear than talking about death 30 years later due to lung cancer. The message containing a fear appeal should offer a way out of the anxiety provoked by the fear appeal. Fear appeals should be combined with suggestions about beneficial behavior that give a positive counter to the fear appeal.

Audience segmentation strategies are very important to campaign success. In addition to looking at demographic statistics and gender differences, message content can be modified appropriately by taking into account the *reference groups* of the target audience. For example, reference groups for girls relative to girls will be different from those for girls relative to boys. Segmentation gives campaign planners a better idea of who they are going to reach with a given set of messages. Campaigns often can reach one segment of an overall audience, such as teenagers, more effectively than others.

Mass media alone cannot reach the majority of high-risk youth in ways that lead to behavioral results. For behavior change, we have to rely primarily on interpersonal strategies, which are both expert based and opinion leader based. Therefore, mass media should be combined with family, school, community, and peer activation strategies. The mass media component can be used to recruit for and to promote interpersonal programs. For instance, media messages can recruit individuals to attend small group training classes for smoking cessation, exercise, and dietary change.

For youth, the first thing to look at are the different interpersonal channels, as well as media channels. It isn't that youth don't connect with the news media, they just watch specialized media, such as MTV, for news about what interests them (rock acts, new recordings, movies, and so on). As yet, we do not have a good understanding about how effective these specialized media could be for messages that promote changing behaviors. In health communication, we have more experience with interpersonal communication through teachers, peers, and institutions such as school. It does seem that one of the more promising uses of mass media is to build a social norm about the desirable behavior. For example, we can create the norm that smoking is not cool through the use of clever PSAs. At the same time, however, we must develop interpersonal skills in our audience that help them resist in situations where peer pressure to smoke is great.

Television cannot change audience behavior directly, but it can create awareness of services, reinforce or provide social norms for health, and show behavior models. Effective strategies take time to design and need feedback for improvement.

What is the most successful mass media campaign to change health behavior you have known, and why do you think it worked?

The Stanford Heart Disease Prevention Program was a successful campaign because it was well organized and well run, and was receptive to input from its audience. The target communities in California were just beginning to change their health behavior patterns anyway at the time the campaign began, so the timing was just right.

What role should federal, state, or local governments play in media campaigns?

Government is the largest provider of funds for public health mass media campaigns. Government-run media campaigns are often guided by the influence of political constituencies, such as anti-drug abuse groups. We have to weigh carefully the costs and the benefits of government involvement in campaigns, however. The government usually gives just enough funds to get a campaign started, but not enough for its completion. If campaign designers rely too heavily on government funding, they can be left out in the cold when the funding runs out, with the whole potential for impact of the campaign jeopardized.

What organizations and organizational factors contribute to the success or failure of media campaigns?

A campaign is likely to be more successful if it has a number of organizations working on it. The involvement of media organizations is a key factor. When funds are inadequate, the messages that finally are broadcast are reduced to the lowest common denominator, so as not to be offensive to those who donate airtime or their constituencies, and thus are weaker in their effects. Grass-roots organizations generally have the ability to run, evaluate, and institutionalize a campaign. All organizations involved in a campaign are also looking for what benefits the campaign will have for them.

What methods would you suggest for financing media campaigns for health?

Funds are available from federal agencies, but many local agencies that want to run media campaigns do not have the capability to apply for those funds. So there is a proliferation of public communication campaigns run by other organizations that can win the funds—none well planned, well evaluated, or well implemented. The result is a misunderstanding about how campaigns *could* work, and a wrong idea about how much effective campaigns really cost.

VICKI FREIMUTH
University of Maryland

ABOUT THE INTERVIEWEE

Vicki Freimuth earned a doctorate from Florida State University and is Director of Health Communication and Professor in the Department of Speech Communication at the University of Maryland, College Park. She teaches courses in health communication, diffusion of innovations, and research methods. Her research focuses on the dissemination of health information in the United States and in developing countries. She is the primary author of *Searching for Health Information* (University of Pennsylvania Press). Her publications have appeared in *Human Communication Research, Journal of Communication, American Journal of Public Health, Health Education Research, Health Education Quarterly,* and *Science, Technology, & Human Values.* She consults regularly for the National Cancer Institute; the National Heart, Lung, and Blood Institute; the National Institute on Alcohol Abuse and Alcoholism; the National Eye Institute; the Office for Substance Abuse Prevention; and the Agency for International Development.

Dr. Freimuth's activities have principally concerned the formative evaluation of media campaigns. She has worked on Office of Cancer Communication campaigns, asbestos awareness campaigns, antismoking campaigns, AIDS communication campaigns, family planning campaigns, and child survival campaigns. Dr. Freimuth has not been involved in any campaigns targeted specifically to high-risk youth. However, she is currently working on a research project on AIDS among college students and also on a project concerned with reducing the cancer knowledge gap among minority audiences, which presents challenges similar to those associated with high-risk youth.

*   *   *

What are the most common reasons mass media campaigns do not achieve their hoped-for results, and what are the most common reasons some campaigns are relatively successful?

One reason for the success of campaigns is their use of formative evaluation. Campaigns are often highly creative and professionally produced, but the messages or the appeals used are inappropriate for the target audience; formative evaluation helps to shape message content. People trained in schools of public health get strong training in summative evaluation methods but little or no formative evaluation training. It flies in the face of their epidemiological study, emphasizing large-scale samples and quantitative work. Targeting audiences is very critical, and we generally go about it in an unsophisticated manner, basing it on such simplistic factors as demographics.

Campaign practitioners often have a kind of blind faith in the potential impact of the mass media. Legislators and government officials think that social problems can be solved if people watch PSAs. Media *can* promote more awareness of an issue, but behavior change can be achieved only through interpersonal interventions. Interpersonal and community-level efforts can be *stimulated* through the media, even on a national level, or through a centralized campaign as shown by the *Chemical People* program on PBS, but these efforts must supplement the media campaign.

We often prepackage information for a target audience without knowing exactly what the information needs of the target audience are and what questions the people are really asking. *People are active information seekers if the information offered is responsive to their needs.* The mass media can be used to stimulate information seeking by a target audience, by letting them know that information they really want is available.

The National Institutes of Health are very print oriented in their health communication efforts, even though it is well known now that print is not a very effective channel for reaching high-risk audiences. The reason lies partly in NIH's concern with accountability: A print message represents a tangible product that permits routine accountability, but the impact is likely to be low.

Before embarking on a media campaign, we should determine whether the problem we want to tackle is even amenable to a communication campaign solution. We may consider a person to blame for a social problem when the solution to the problem may lie entirely outside of the individual's control. We tend to overlook the environment of our target audience and the constraints that are operating on these individuals, often preventing them from changing their behavior no matter how persuasive the message.

Government officials know that to reach minorities in the United States they must use community-based approach and strategies. But these officials have their own constraints, such as insufficient staff. Federal officials are mandated to reach everybody, but it is difficult or impossible for one office, with a centralized program, to reach out effectively to many communities at the same time. So some communities simply get neglected.

How could present health communication campaign models be improved to make them useful for planning, implementing, and evaluating mass media campaigns?

Public communication models, such as the social marketing model, the health belief model, and social modeling theory, are difficult to use because these are "explanatory models," structured from the individual's point of view. They do not deal with the operating reality of the campaign.

Existing models are therefore helpful to researchers, but not to campaign designers. More change agent-oriented models are needed. The current models are generally inadequate to give guidance to the actual process of campaign planning. There is one exception to this observation: The social marketing model is controversial and has limitations, but it does offer a process view, a series of practical guidelines, a sequence of suggested activities, and a systematic methodology, and it is change agent oriented.

The overall problem is that of *synthesizing* the various models for promoting health behavior change through campaigns. In research, the models are treated as very isolated, but actually they are not. A theoretical synthesis might be feasible. When we try to integrate the models, we find contradictions. That is when many practitioners give up and say that none of the models is workable! We have to show practitioners how the different models can be used as they move through the process of a campaign. We have to translate academic research into practical guide-lines and extract from the research something helpful to practitioners. This includes dealing with the contradictions in a practical way.

What roles can formative or summative evaluation play in the relative success of a health communication campaign?

We lose many opportunities to learn from summative evaluations of campaigns. Summative evaluation is done in a very specific way, and a lot more can be learned from it besides finding out whether the campaign met its objectives. We have not extracted enough from the findings of the evaluations that have been done up to now. We should be able to extract quite specific and generalizable principles from summative evaluations.

The importance of formative evaluation is understood, but it is not often used because it is not respected as a research method. It does not adhere to the traditional research methodology of large samples and so on. Formative evaluation also is perceived as time-consuming. Funding agencies tend to channel funds toward actual interventions, even when we do not know whether or not the campaigns are effective.

What are the unique characteristics and special difficulties of preventive health communication campaigns, especially those aimed at high-risk youth?

Preventive health campaigns are difficult because often there are no obvious rewards for adoption of the preventive behavior. Young people, for instance, almost always think they are very healthy, do not need to worry about any disease, and have no immediate health concerns. Thus they don't see rewards coming from the changes in behavior that campaigns advocate.

Campaigns have dealt with this problem by looking for immediate rewards associated with preventive behavior. Youth are at a stage of life where they are highly likely to take risks. Youth have a feeling of invulnerability, they lack personalization of the risk, and sometimes campaigns inadvertently reinforce these feelings. Many people who plan and execute campaigns are white, middle-class professionals who are ignorant of the target groups they are trying to reach. Involvement of the minority media and of minority professionals is necessary for successful campaigns aimed at such minorities, and involvement of youth is needed for campaigns targeted to youth.

How do factors such as age groupings, fear appeals, audience segmentation, and use of opinion leaders contribute to the design of mass media campaigns targeted to high-risk youth?

A national high blood pressure media campaign started with strong fear appeals, then stopped using such appeals, and recently started again using some modest fear appeals. Such strategy changes are difficult because they interfere with other aspects of a campaign's operation, since people have such strong reactions to fear. Fear appeal messages should at least present some way of resolving the fear. Fear messages also have to be very different for different audience segments, since both what is feared and how fear is responded to may be very different for various groups.

Public service announcements suffer from the problem of nonavailability of appropriate broadcasting time slots, at least for free airtime. Campaigns often overuse print media and underuse radio. We dismiss radio as an ineffective channel because it does not show up when we ask people where they obtained their information from a health campaign, but we know radio is an important force in the lives of many people, especially those in minority communities. Direct mail is used more and more in communication campaigns.

We have to broaden our concept of channels as ways to reach people when information is needed by them. We have to think about the points in time and the environments in which people are really going to want information. Then we have to offer capsuled snippets of information that are useful at those points in time and places. For example, a supermarket nutrition program that had "supermarket talkers" to discuss nutrition, and in which products were labeled with the required nutritional information, was very successful.

KIPLING J. GALLION
The University of Texas at Austin

ABOUT THE INTERVIEWEE

Kipling J. Gallion is Communication Coordinator for Media Research and Production, South Texas Health Research Center, University of Texas Health Science Center, San Antonio. He is currently Co-Principal Investigator for the Substance Abuse Video Series for Hispanic Adolescents, sponsored by the Office for Substance Abuse Prevention; Regional Medical Producer for Salud: Mexican-American Participation in Cancer Prevention, funded by the National Cancer Institute; Co-Investigator for Programa a Su Salud, for the South Texas Health Research Center; and Investigator for Public Relations Planning to Promote Services to Minorities with Disabilities, sponsored by the Administration of Development Disabilities, U.S. Department of Health and Human Services. He has also served as a health communications and media consultant to such organizations as the Entertainment Industries Council; the National Heart, Lung, and Blood Institute; Project Reach (Austin, Texas); and the American Heart Association.

Before coming to The University of Texas in 1987, Gallion worked as Video Producer and Editor for Video Arts Production in Austin, Texas; was Video Production Instructor in the Department of Communication at Stanford University; and served as Producer of *Peninsula Weekly* for KCSM-TV, San Mateo, California. From 1977 to 1979, he was a Peace Corps volunteer in Jamaica, West Indies.

Dr. Gallion is the author or coauthor of a number of publications and presentations and the producer-author of a series of weekly preventive health media programs and other video productions. He has produced smoking-cessation motivational films for the University of Colombia, and is currently involved in a youth campaign oriented to alcohol and other drug abuse, teenage pregnancy, and smoking. He received his Ph.D. in communication research in 1991 from The University of Texas at Austin.

*   *   *

What are the most common reasons mass media campaigns do not achieve their hoped-for results, and what are the most common reasons some campaigns are relatively successful?

The mass media can be effective in achieving knowledge and attitude change, but if the objective of a campaign is behavior change, then an interpersonal component must be seriously considered. The chances for impact are much greater if there is an interpersonal dimension to supplement the media component.

The effective management of the whole campaign is very important. Unsuccessful campaigns usually do not have individuals who can interact effectively between the media producers and social science investigators, and the campaigns may falter greatly as a result.

How could present health communication campaign models be improved to make them useful for planning, implementing, and evaluating mass media campaigns?

Most theoretical models dealing with public communication campaigns are actually fairly similar in their basic assumptions about human behavior. Social marketing, social learning theory, and the diffusion of innovation paradigm can all be useful in designing campaigns.

Many high-risk youth groups simply do not attend to the mass media. Because of their life-styles, they are not tuned in at the times that campaign messages are broadcast or they have nontraditional media habits. We can overcome this problem in part by creating focused media, such as video- or audiocassettes, and distributing them interpersonally or through small social networks including high-risk groups. Youth in high-risk groups can be reached effectively through a range of "small media" such as tabloids, booklets, comic books, and audiotapes featuring individuals like themselves or local celebrities.

What roles can formative or summative evaluation play in the relative success of a health communication campaign?

Formative research is critical to the success of a media campaign. In a fast-changing world, we cannot rely on assumptions, even those of "experts," to create and implement a campaign. We must pretest campaign materials in pilot projects, with focus groups, and in interview surveys to find ways of reducing barriers to campaign messages.

There is a problem with measurement in general, but with summative research of campaigns specifically. The problem is how to gauge the success of something that is not simply behavior change. Summative evaluation should look at the whole process of system change that supports modification of health behavior, and not just at the behavior of the target audience. For example, in large programs where the efforts of many groups are being synthesized, summative evaluation can measure the number of volunteers the program was able to draw from the target community, the number of role models enlisted, contacts within the medical community, development of community advocacy activity, and increase in volunteer activities of other agencies. These measures of impact are important for understanding *what* happened and *why* it happened.

What are the unique characteristics and special difficulties of preventive health communication campaigns, especially those aimed at high-risk youth?

The main difficulty with prevention campaigns is that we are asking people to change what they are doing *now*, while the positive aspects of health protection are long term. The negative impacts of current health habits are felt sometime in the future, often the remote future. Usually the communities we are targeting are disadvantaged. They do not have the resources to overcome environmental constraints to solve their social problems. To be successful, media campaigns have to address economic problems, social problems, bigotry, and racism.

Often media campaigns are funded by agencies that high-risk individuals have grown to distrust. From the target community's viewpoint, stigma is associated with outside people coming into a community and telling the people there what to do. When targeting high-risk adolescents, we must be especially aware of deep-seated, long-standing psychological and emotional barriers to campaign messages.

How do factors such as age groupings, fear appeals, audience segmentation, and use of opinion leaders contribute to the design of mass media campaigns targeted to high-risk youth?

Adolescent to early teenage years (9 to 15 years) are a good time to target campaigns, because at this age youth have only limited life experience, they are establishing behaviors more than at a younger or an older age, and they are building individual identities. So they can be highly receptive to the right message delivered the right way. From the perspective of social modeling, role models are more effective if they are one to three years older than members of the target audience.

Fear appeals do not seem to work well for attitude or behavior change, although youthful audiences will often *say* they need to be shocked by hearing the true risks involved. Fear appeals can heighten awareness when there is an absolute void of knowledge about an issue. Usually there is not enough message time to overcome the potential negative effects of fear appeals, and therefore great care must be exercised if fear or shock is part of a message. Long-term learning needs positive reinforcement, not negative reinforcement, which is what fear appeals provide.

Audience segmentation strategies are extremely important. We must understand audience needs and where the audience stands with regard to the particular issue. We also need baseline knowledge of attitudes and behaviors, so that resources can be used in an effective way to fashion appropriate messages.

Opinion leaders, another valuable component of any intervention, can be identified by looking carefully in the target community. Which students are prominent and in high-profile yet salient positions in school, athletics, school government, or creative activities?

When possible, monetary incentives should not be made an issue with opinion leaders. Such precedents are not worthwhile to set up, because we cannot repay the time and energy the leaders put voluntarily into projects— there is not that much money available! This should not preclude creative thinking about other types of incentives. The best incentive may be the very reason such people get interested in the campaign issue in the first place: We can show in a tangible way how their efforts are contributing to the welfare of their community. Also, such incentives as certificates of recognition, picnics, and an annual gala dinner may be offered.

As an incentive for youth to be involved in campaigns, it might be a good idea to show them the benefits of *meeting new people*, such as opinion leaders. We can show that by developing a new little social circle and creating a new social network they can make new (and maybe better) friends and relationships, and also get information about better employment opportunities or community activities. This can be a powerful motivator for campaign participation.

Radio is an effective communication channel for youth because it is mobile. A radio can be carried around everywhere a teenager goes, even by car. Music is a very powerful influence in a young person's life. Print media also can be effective if they meet the entertainment criteria of the target audience. Television is not as effective, and carrying a variety of messages over TV may not be as cost-effective as using radio to disseminate those messages.

We need to develop a "community participation model" for mass media health campaigns. We have to develop volunteer networks within the target community itself that can distribute small media such as comic books, tabloids, and audiotapes. Unless we have these volunteer individuals integrated with the high-risk groups almost on an equal level, the high-risk target groups are not going to pay sufficient attention to the messages.

What is the most successful mass media campaign to change health behavior you have known, and why do you think it worked?

Programa a Su Salud, at the South Texas Health Research Center, UTHSC in San Antonio, University of Texas, is a successful campaign that is community based. There is wide awareness of the campaign, as many target community individuals know the campaign practitioners personally. Another reason for its success is the way the campaign messages are framed. "Role models" or individuals in the community who change their behavior are featured in the media. These individuals are shown living healthier life-styles and exhibiting greater control over their social environments. This strategy is different from someone in the medical community dictating to young people what their behavior should be. The community feels responsible for the campaign messages and thus feels "ownership" of the messages.

What role should federal, state, or local governments play in media campaigns?

While the federal government has some money to fund media campaigns, state and local governments are important for giving credence to the organization undertaking a campaign. Without the support of local health departments, for instance, most health-related campaigns would be very difficult to undertake. There also is more competition in the health information field today, with a conflict of private interests and public interests. People and institutions may feel threatened when a new organization comes along. Involving the existing agencies with a stake in the health issue a new organization wants to address can be critical. Local governments are especially helpful in the initial phases of campaign operation, and can help in getting connections within the target communities. Also, if the program is successful, the replication of the program model can best be shouldered by the government or other health agencies.

What organizations or organizational factors contribute to the success or failure of media campaigns?

Organizational factors do significantly affect the success of media campaigns. Most campaign designers cannot interact effectively with both commercial media representatives and social science investigators. The researchers are simply not aware of the business conditions that drive the media business. The mass media industry is constantly evolving:

Individual broadcast personalities change, allegiances and formats change. If these quickly changing aspects of the media business are not closely monitored, there is little likelihood of forming a durable partnership with the media industry. The primary concern of the industry is not research or social good. Commercial media campaigns are interested in the bottom line of how the campaigns will help their business and profitability.

Another important reason for a program's success is the way stories are presented to broadcasters. In the Texas project already mentioned, the stories are presented from the human-interest angle, so that success stories are shown every week. Whatever the message may be, it has to be presented in an entertaining format that is exciting to the target audience. The narrative must be on an equal footing with the health content. Striking the proper balance between entertainment and health information is a constant challenge, but it can also be the most interesting aspect of media production!

We have to learn to build alliances and coalitions (and not "empires"). For example, we have to garner the support of local clinics, nurses, private physicians, and other health practitioners serving target communities. They are prime enabling agents for the project, particularly at the street and community level. They are crucial in locating role models. We have to fashion messages that develop consensus rather than conflict with the various individual actors and agencies involved. This includes the professional groups representing the health professionals just mentioned.

Developing coalitions with the media can help reduce campaign costs. If the media campaign can be made attractive enough, if formative research is done well, if the needs of the media industry can be anticipated, then there is a good chance of forming a lasting partnership with the media industry and of getting significant amounts of contributed airtime, labor, and other resources.

ROBERT W. GILLESPIE
Population Communications

ABOUT THE INTERVIEWEE

As President and founder of Population Communications, Robert Gillespie authored the "Statement on Population Stabilization," which has since been signed by 48 heads of government. In the 10 largest underdeveloped countries, Population Communications has contracted with motion picture scriptwriters to develop screenplays with themes aimed at improving the status of women, lowering infant mortality, and achieving the small family goal. Working with prominent demographers and economists, Population Communications publishes books and promotes awareness of the population problem among national and international leaders.

Prior to the founding of Population Communications in 1978, Gillespie provided assistance to the Bangladesh government in designing a national sterilization plan of action, and served with the Population Council as Assistant Director of Information and Education in its New York office, and as the Council Representative in Taiwan and Iran. Gillespie has produced two documentary films and is the author of a number of books, reports, and articles on population planning. He has served on the boards of directors and advisory committees for such organizations as the Population Institute, Zero Population Growth, the World Health Organization, the UNESCO Family Planning Communication Research Committee, and the International Committee on Applied Research in Population. He received his B.S. in social sciences and economics from California Polytechnic State University and an MPH in population planning from the University of Michigan.

*   *   *

What are the most common reasons mass media campaigns do not achieve their hoped-for results, and what are the most common reasons some campaigns are relatively successful?

For a campaign to be successful, the messages should be pretested thoroughly. The basic message must be repeated over time and, if possible, in a number of media. The messages should provide specific information, permitting the target audience to respond with specific behaviors—for example, post office box numbers to write to, phone numbers to call, or places to go for services. The audience wants to know both negative and positive aspects of a new behavior, so the message should portray all relevant aspects of the new behavior in an honest way. Community follow-through with one-on-one as well as group interactions also are important.

How could present health communication campaign models be improved to make them useful for planning, implementing, and evaluating mass media campaigns?

Theoretical campaign models are generally adequate. But they could be improved by more fully incorporating the experiences of private companies in selling consumer products; social marketing offers much potential for enhancing media campaigns for health.

What roles can formative or summative evaluation play in the relative success of a health communication campaign?

Formative evaluation is crucial for a mass media health campaign to be effective. Pretest audience surveys are absolutely necessary to know the demeanor of the target audience before beginning to disseminate a message, as well as to understand the initial impact the message has.

How do factors such as age groupings, fear appeals, audience segmentation, and use of opinion leaders contribute to the design of mass media campaigns targeted to high-risk youth?

Peer pressure is a very important factor in determining the health behaviors of youth. Also, youth respond better when youth talk to them than when older adults do so, whether in person or through media messages.

Musical forms of communication can be highly effective for young people. Radio also is an important channel of communication for youth audiences. The criterion for determining the media mix should be the cost-effectiveness of each communication channel, and a good campaign includes a way of making this determination fairly systematically.

Fear appeals in and of themselves may not be effective, but fear elements often need to be included in a media campaign in the sense that the negative aspects of the health issue should also be conveyed to the audience. However, positive incentives are critically important in a media campaign, since they provide a rationalization for the audience that there is something in the behavior change for them.

Mass media and interpersonal communication strategies go hand in hand in health campaigns. Mass communication strategies, in addition to providing knowledge to the audience, serve the important function of legitimating the role of grass-roots workers who typically offer and coordinate the interpersonal activities in a campaign.

What is the most successful mass media campaign to change health behavior you have known, and why do you think it worked?

The Isfahan (Iran) communication campaign for family planning was very successful. It used multimedia, multichannel messages through radio, television, newspapers, magazines, flip charts, film clips in cinema houses, and direct mail. The mass media interventions were combined with door-to-door visits by health and family planning workers, and group meetings of the target audience were organized.

Smoking-cessation campaigns in the United States also are among the most successful. These campaigns concentrate on multiple distribution systems, they have great autonomy, and they have developed effective collaborations with the mass media, for example, for significant donated print and electronic media dissemination of their messages.

What role should federal, state, or local governments play in media campaigns?

Working with government agencies in a productive way is crucial to a media campaign's success. This is especially true if the media outlets themselves are controlled by the government, as they are in many Third World nations. Campaign designers from the United States must understand this reality if they are to work effectively in such Third World countries.

What methods would you suggest for financing media campaigns for health?

One way to produce innovative financing for mass media health campaigns is to provide a *salable product* as part of the campaign—a recording, a videocassette, a poster, or the like. More important, we must concentrate on maximizing the cost-effectiveness of campaigns by careful planning and allocation of resources. If a campaign is cost-effective, the financial savings can be used to fund other campaigns.

ROBERT HORNIK
University of Pennsylvania

ABOUT THE INTERVIEWEE

Robert Hornik is Professor of Communication and Director of the Center for International Health and Development Communication at the

Annenberg School for Communication at the University of Pennsylvania. He is the principal investigator for several ongoing research studies and evaluations of large-scale health communication programs in developing countries and in the United States. His most recent book is *Development Communication: Information, Agriculture and Nutrition in the Third World* (Longman, 1988). He earned a Ph.D. in communication research from Stanford University.

Dr. Hornik has designed and evaluated mass media health campaigns in Third World countries. He has not been involved in campaigns specifically targeted to high-risk youth.

* * *

What are the most common reasons mass media campaigns do not achieve their hoped-for results, and what are the most common reasons some campaigns are relatively successful?

Reach is a major problem in many mass media campaigns. Many campaigns do not get through to the intended audience, certainly not to the extent required, and what is achieved is unimpressive. This reach problem is encountered more often in campaigns that rely wholly on interpersonal channels, which are very difficult to organize. Interpersonal channels have definite advantages, but as a practical problem, not many people possess the know-how to organize these channels properly.

Those who develop mass media health campaigns often do not really understand their audiences. Many times creative people get together and decide that they have a great way of reaching a particular target audience. Sometimes they are right, but often what they are doing may not be responsive to the target audience's needs and interests, and, if so, the campaign will fail.

We cannot demand of audience members what they simply cannot do, not because of lack of motivation, but because they lack the ability required due to environmental constraints. The attitude that a message designer would like an audience or individual to adopt involves encoding a knowledge objective into a message. This is usually done from the point of view of the designer, not that of the audience. Corporate marketing efforts, for instance, are more sophisticated than mass media health campaigns in translating concepts and objectives into effective campaign messages that fit the vision and beliefs of the audience/consumer.

Other factors affecting the relative success of campaigns are putting optimum resources into the campaign, defining correctly the audience's behavioral patterns, and finding out under what conditions messages coming externally to a social system exert influence on that system.

How could present health communication campaign models be improved to make them useful for planning, implementing, and evaluating mass media campaigns?

All models of public communication campaigns are defined in terms of the essential steps that one goes through. Theoretically, the models seem excellent. But the problem comes when their practicability is tested. The problem is not with the theoretical basis for the models, but that in practice they do not work that well.

What roles can formative or summative evaluation play in the relative success of a health communication campaign?

Usually the data collected in formative evaluation research are not turned into a detailed plan of action. There is no clear planning process *before* data collection, and the data are gathered for their own sake, without hypotheses to guide the data-collection effort itself. Nor are there any a priori expectations that would make the data collection flexible and more responsive to the needs of the campaign objectives. Formative evaluation is conducted mechanically, and because of the lack of strategic planning the data collected are not very relevant and thus don't get utilized.

What are the unique characteristics and special difficulties of preventive health communication campaigns, especially those aimed at high-risk youth?

The models used for public communication campaigns have a strong individual psychological basis: All the models deal with individuals moving from some earlier stage to some later stage of development. This view may be incorrect. What appears to be individual behavior may really be social behavior (with the individual behaviors very responsive to social expectations). The cognitive stages in the models may be an effect, rather than the cause, of overt behavior change. The behavior may come first, then one may cognitively think about it because social decisions (as opposed to isolated individual decisions) are made at this point. So the behavior change model in a campaign should be independent of the individual cognitive change model. Effective campaigns should stress group and social norms. We should try to link the individual to his or her social environment, and try to create a "group change" rather than an individual change. Unfortunately, not many campaigns have been strategized this way.

The essential problem of campaigns is getting the target audience to see that the campaign is encouraging them to solve a problem *they already perceive as important.* The campaign should advocate a solution about a problem that the audience already perceives for itself. For drug abuse, many people do not perceive a drug's nonuse as a solution for any problem that they have. If we are not solving any problem for the audience, they are not going to listen to our solutions.

How do factors such as age groupings, fear appeals, audience segmentation, and use of opinion leaders contribute to the design of mass media campaigns targeted to high-risk youth?

Fear appeals seem to work in some circumstances for some sorts of messages, but not in other settings, as the literature and recent research show. Thus it is *always* questionable whether a fear-based appeal should be part of a campaign.

Audience segmentation approaches assume that different messages work best for different subpopulations. Actually, there is not much empirical evidence to suggest that different messages work for different groups, or even whether any messages work at all for high-risk youth.

It is not very certain as to whether high-risk youth groups have opinion leaders at all, in the sense of clearly identifiable people who are particularly influential with other people in that group. However, if we are taking a group norm strategy as opposed to an individual cognition theory in designing a mass media campaign, then getting the same message consistently through a lot of channels is quite important. Youth will hear the same message from the mass media, from their health people, and from school, and there may be a synergistic effect.

An incentive/disincentive strategy depends on the kinds of incentives we want to use—and includes determining whether the incentives/ disincentives selected can be applied ethically, legally, constitutionally, and in the prevailing social climate. The audience has to be studied carefully in order to find out the best incentives to use, and to understand their effects on the target audience. First, we must know whether we are rewarding the target audience for solving a problem that they themselves want to resolve in the first place. An incentive strategy will work only if the answer is yes.

Using multiple media channels is important for campaign success. The more the audience comes to believe that a particular behavior is the expected behavior in their social group, the more they will tend toward it, and multiple channels for message delivery can help to create this expectation. But usually there is a trade-off: The more messages are perfected for one channel, the less money there will be for messages sent through other channels. The reach of a campaign in a condition of scarce resources is an important issue; we cannot do a project brilliantly in one school and not bother about replicability. The question of deciding the various channels is a practical one, rather than a theoretical one.

No one would dispute that a good "field agent" is very effective in the community portion of any campaign. In practice, however, many field agents are not highly motivated, and thus may not have much impact.

Mass media channels have the potential to accomplish much more than they are usually credited with. The timing for a mass media message is important. For example, if a child is dying of diarrhea and television or radio gives directions for using oral rehydration therapy (ORT), the mother may directly alter her behavior by following the instructions given. If the mass media are clear about what behavior they are recommending and are solving a problem that the target audience perceives, people will often change their behaviors fairly quickly. The notion of an immense resistance to change, overcome only by sustained interpersonal communication, may not always be true.

What role should federal, state, or local governments play in media campaigns?

Only government has the kind of money required for long-term public communication campaigns, with the funding depending, of course, on whether the government believes that a certain socially desirable behavior should be advocated. There are many problems in working with a large government entity, of course, but this is usually the only choice for large-scale campaigns.

At the local levels of government, the amount of money available is smaller and the talent pool is reduced, but local governments are adept at activating effective community channels. The problem is to determine at what level campaign activity can be most effectively organized. One way of conducting campaigns would be to have a centralized production of materials and programs at the federal level, and leave the implementation to local agencies.

JOSE RUBEN JARA
Institute for Communication Research

ABOUT THE INTERVIEWEE

Jose Ruben Jara is Director of the Institute for Communication Research, a private research organization in Mexico City. He has directed evaluation research projects to determine the effects of communication campaigns to prevent adolescent pregnancy and AIDS. For instance, he headed the evaluation research project that measured the effects of the song "Cuando Estemos Juntos," by Tatiana and Johnny. He has also conducted research on prosocial television soap operas in Mexico that are intended to promote adult literacy, family planning, and female equality.

Dr. Jara received his undergraduate degree from the Universidad Iberoamericana in Mexico City, and then earned his Ph.D. in communication from Michigan State University. After teaching communication at the Universidad Iberoamericana, he founded the Institute for Communication Research in 1982.

*   *   *

What are the most common reasons mass media campaigns do not achieve their hoped-for results, and what are the most common reasons some campaigns are relatively successful?

A problem confronting communication scholars and campaign designers is their lack of communication with each other and their failure to work together as a *team*. Mass media campaigns often communicate messages that do not adequately reflect what the audience wants or how it thinks. Moreover, the expected results of these campaigns are often ill defined, unrealistic, or so broad that they cannot be measured even if they happen. One variable crucial to the success of all communication campaigns is the quality and level of talent input. However, talent i difficult to define, pinpoint, and control.

A soft-sell, subtle approach helps increase the likelihood that a campaign will be effective. The entertainment-education strategy of the Tatiana and Johnny campaign in Mexico was an example of this approach. Also, the personnel providing the infrastructure (such as teen age contraceptive clinics) need to be aware of campaign objectives, so as to be prepared to provide the services that clients will request Otherwise, the campaign will just create frustrated audience members who try to follow through with behavior change but can't.

How could present health communication campaign models be im proved to make them useful for planning, implementing, and evaluating mass media campaigns?

Theoretical models for communication campaigns provide only very general guidelines for developing good campaigns. These models must be supplemented with the experience of practitioners and verified by actual campaigns and their results. Models usually are more helpful in the evaluation phase of a campaign than they are in the planning and implementation phases.

What roles can formative or summative evaluation play in the relative success of a health communication campaign?

More formative evaluation is needed in media campaigns, so as to better determine the role models with which the audience identifies, and thereby the actors/singers/speakers who will be most compatible with campaign goals. This type of evaluation can also reveal the audience's feelings about the particular issue being treated in the campaign. Focus groups are a particularly critical component of formative evaluation, and can address both role model and health issue concerns of the intended target audiences

What are the unique characteristics and special difficulties of preven tive health communication campaigns, especially those aimed at high risk youth?

Evaluation research for the Tatiana and Johnny campaign, and for a recent AIDS prevention project in Mexico, showed that the more at risk the audience is with respect to the health subject presented in the campaign, the more likely it is that the audience will be influenced by the campaign. In both these studies, there was an increased probability of behavioral change among high-risk individuals as a result of exposure to the campaign. The conclusion: Self-perceived risk is related to behavioral change, and campaigns need to be designed around this central finding or they will not be successful.

How do factors such as age groupings, fear appeals, audience segmentation, and use of opinion leaders contribute to the design of mass media campaigns targeted to high-risk youth?

The specific age group to target in campaigns varies according to the issue presented. High-risk youth tend to simply block out fear appeals psychologically. An element of humor in messages may provide a better way to persuade high-risk individuals.

The target audience is actually a mosaic of subaudiences, with drastic differences among them. Audience segmentation strategies are therefore crucial to campaign success, and multiple subsegments even within specific target audiences must be identified.

The greatest incentive for young people to adopt a certain behavior is to make this behavior socially fashionable. Peer acceptance and group belonging are considerably more important to youth than are economic considerations or long-term health consequences.

Interpersonal communication is the most suitable channel to initiate behavioral change, because this channel provides an emotional element that makes the messages more powerful. Mass media are used to create the social climate, and then the campaign issue is clarified through interpersonal communication. The most effective media mix depends on the issue to be presented. In general, radio is more popular among youth than is television.

What is the most successful mass media campaign to change health behavior you have known, and why do you think it worked?

The most successful campaigns in Mexico center on educational soap operas. They are broadcast over several months, for one hour each workday in prime time. The emotional melodrama in these programs evokes strong audience identification and involvement with the protagonists. The television soap operas achieve high audience ratings and provide many opportunities for delivering health messages.

What role should federal, state, or local governments play in media campaigns?

The governments in developing countries play a key role in communication campaigns, because they have the essential resources. The private sector in these countries should expand its participation in campaigns, but has not yet done so very often.

What organizations and organizational factors contribute to the success or failure of media campaigns?

One organizational factor crucial to campaign success is strong, interested *leadership* by people in top positions in relevant organizations. In Latin America, the right connections with the right people and organizations help a campaign immensely. An example of this was the boost the Tatiana and Johnny campaign got from being launched by Raul Velasco of Televisa on his extremely popular Sunday afternoon television variety program. Because of this program, an estimated 150 million people in Latin America viewed the first performance of "When We Are Together."

What methods would you suggest for financing media campaigns for health?

Mixing an educational theme with entertainment is a general strategy for financing mass media campaigns, as with the best-selling Tatiana and Johnny record. Corporate sponsorship is also a viable strategy; corporate underwriting requires that the campaign message not be highly controversial, however, and that there be a societal consensus regarding the issue presented in the campaign and the need to do something about it. A key strategy in any entertainment-education campaign is first to achieve popularity, and then connect the campaign's educational message to the entertainment.

C. ANDERSON JOHNSON
University of Southern California

ABOUT THE INTERVIEWEE

C. Anderson Johnson is Director of the Institute for Health Promotion and Disease Prevention Research, School of Medicine, University of

Southern California. He also is Director of the Division of Health Behavior Research, Department of Preventive Medicine, USC School of Medicine; Associate Professor of Preventive Medicine, School of Medicine, USC: and Sidney Garfield Chair in Health Science (Preventive Medicine). He has also served as Assistant Professor and Co-Director, Program in Cardiovascular Behavior, College of Pharmacy and School of Public Health, University of Minnesota, and as Project Director and Research Psychologist for the U.S. National Bureau of Standards.

Dr. Johnson has coauthored more than 90 journal articles, including "Prevention of Cigarette Smoking: Three Year Follow-Up of an Educational Program for Youth" (*Surgeon General's Report on Smoking & Health: Cancer*, 1982), "Viewing and Evaluation of a Televised Drug Education Program by Students Previously or Concurrently Exposed or Not Exposed to School-Based Substance Abuse Prevention Programs" (*Health Education Research*, 1987), and "The Television, School, and Family Smoking Prevention/Cessation Project: IV. Controlling for Program Success Expectancies Across Experimental and Control Conditions" (*Addictive Behavior*, 1989).

Dr. Johnson received his Ph.D. in social psychology from Duke University in 1974. He has designed and evaluated broadcast television, school-based, and community-based campaigns for smoking cessation and prevention. These programs have been targeted to high-risk youth in the Los Angeles area and in Kansas City and Indianapolis.

* * *

What are the most common reasons mass media campaigns do not achieve their hoped-for results, and what are the most common reasons some campaigns are relatively successful?

Among the chief reasons mass media health campaigns do not achieve their hoped-for results is that there is a lack of real quality implementation, a lack of follow-through on this implementation, and a lack of adequate evaluation research (both formative and summative). Campaigns that are based on well-established approaches to prevention, that impart resistance skills training, that try to mobilize social influence, and that monitor implementation closely, utilize feedback, and create community mechanisms for long-term maintenance of the changed behavior are most likely to be successful.

How could present health communication campaign models be improved to make them useful for planning, implementing, and evaluating mass media campaigns?

For the typical campaign designer or implementer, the theoretical models of public communication do not seem to be adequate for guiding campaigns. The models have not been adequately described, in the sense that the underlying theory has not been clearly specified and tied to campaign actions.

Communities are dynamic and they are constantly changing. The results of the summative evaluation of a campaign in one community are certainly replicable in other places. But they have to be suitably modified through formative evaluation in the new system. Subgroups change, needs change, beliefs change, and motivating factors operating on the audience change. So appropriate communication channels for reaching the target audience will not be the same from one campaign to another.

Formative evaluation is required to track how messages are reaching the target audience. For example, when replicating the Kansas City project STAR (a highly successful drug abuse prevention campaign) in Indianapolis, it was found that a formative evaluation of the target audience was essential. The I-STAR campaign in Indianapolis has importantly modified the approaches used in the Kansas City campaign, and is more likely to be a success as a result.

What are the unique characteristics and special difficulties of preventive health communication campaigns, especially those aimed at high-risk youth?

Prevention campaigns may be seen by the target audience as "trying to fix something that is not broken." To fix heart disease or to fix drug abuse does not make much sense to the target audience when such problems are not yet perceived as important. Getting youth to attend to prevention is difficult. They see themselves as immune to health problems. Youth do not often see people dying from disease, unlike middle-aged men who see their friends die. The challenge of working with youth is to tap needs that are perceived by the youth. It may not be necessary even to discuss health needs if such needs are not considered salient or of high priority by youth. More important may be social needs, such as acceptance by peers. One of the mistakes of youth campaigns is their focus on health behavior outcomes that are more salient to adults than to youth. By contrast, legislators also do not care about prevention, but for different reasons. They are more excited about rehabilitation, about fixing up people who are already broken. It is not so exciting to work with people who do not have a visible problem that can be corrected.

How do factors such as age groupings, fear appeals, audience segmentation, and use of opinion leaders contribute to the design of mass media campaigns targeted to high-risk youth?

One has to pay attention to what media channels different age groups attend to, and at what age a teenager is most vulnerable to the onset of a particular risk behavior. Drug abuse campaigns should aim at the age group of 11-12-13 years, when the drug threat is first emerging in most communities.

There is little evidence to suggest that fear appeals produce consistently positive campaign results. Fear appeals therefore should be avoided as much as possible in mass media campaigns.

Audience segmentation strategies are extremely important in health campaigns. Certain objectives may be attained without segmentation, but when we try to encourage specific behavioral responses—for example, with the use of role models—we have to pay attention closely to who the audience is, who they identify with, and what their needs are.

Youth peer leaders have been identified through peer nomination in precisely defined targeted communities (such as a school). Another approach is to use celebrities, but one must be very careful because this strategy can easily backfire. The media are quick to expose celebrities if they indulge in some behavior contrary to the ideal. For example, a rock musician who spoke out against alcoholism was arrested for drunk driving and instantly lost credibility with the target audience. Peer models who attract the target audience may be more helpful in campaigns for high-risk youth.

Data from the Kansas City and Indianapolis drug prevention projects conducted by the University of Southern California suggest that the most compelling mediators of program effectiveness seem to be components designed to increase *efficacy and skills*, to enhance the *perception of normative beliefs* with regard to what the normal person is doing, and to create the perception that *avoidance of drug use* is what most kids are trying to do. The mediator found especially powerful is the perception of possible social and peer sanctions if one engages in drug use. To the extent that a campaign can create the perception that peers disapprove of drug use, the campaign will be effective.

Another mediator is positive beliefs about behavioral outcomes (for example, the perceived positive disinhibiting effects of alcohol use). Beliefs about the negative consequences of drug use do not seem to be effective in explaining individual behavior change in Kansas City and Indianapolis. Increased confidence in one's own communication skills seems to mediate campaign effects for use of some particular drugs. Surprisingly, our data show that beliefs about self-efficacy do not mediate behavioral outcomes.

Communication messages and channels that facilitate youth getting together, or that create the illusion of youth getting together, to form a consensus have the most effect on youth. The consensus-generating effect when the audience comes to believe that a particular behavior (for example, drug abuse) is a health problem can be highly effective.

Any single media channel is doomed to failure in the long run. A mix of all available channels is required for a successful campaign. For example, television, radio, billboards, school-based programs, and community organization and activities should be combined in a health campaign.

What role should federal, state, or local governments play in media campaigns?

Governments should fund, give other kinds of support, and, as important, should require that the campaigns they fund contain elements that will increase the likelihood of campaign success. The government should not waste resources on PSAs or other isolated activities, but should support comprehensive campaigns that are based on theory and research, and that provide for feedback and adequate monitoring.

MARCY KELLY
Mediascope

ABOUT THE INTERVIEWEE

Marcy Kelly, President of Mediascope, in Studio City, California, is a film producer and media consultant. She has developed, written, and produced a variety of radio, television, and print public service campaigns on topics including AIDS prevention, drug abuse prevention, birth control, food labeling, and product safety. She has worked for both government and private nonprofit organizations. Positions she has held include President of Woodbine Communications, Executive Director of the Scott Newman Foundation, Media Coordinator for the White House Domestic Policy Staff, Deputy Director for Communications at the National Institute on Drug Abuse, and Press Officer for the Food and Drug Administration. Most recently she produced Musicians for Life, a television and radio public service campaign on AIDS funded by Warner Communications.

*   *   *

What are the most common reasons mass media campaigns do not achieve their hoped-for results, and what are the most common reasons some campaigns are relatively successful?

One reason many campaigns do not achieve their hoped-for results is that there is too much reliance on PSAs. The times for airing PSAs on television cannot be controlled, and the fight for free airtime is very competitive. Radio, and to some extent television, increasingly does not take any public service announcements. Those concerned with the funding of mass media campaigns are "stuck in the groove" of producing PSAs. They too often lack the creative thinking needed to find ways to use other channels. If we look at the demographics of television viewers, we know that different people watch at different times. We also know that teenagers watch much less television than do other groups. But still we spend our money on PSAs, often airing them at times when the target audiences do not even watch television.

I really believe it is time to create a new kind of public service announcement. I don't know what form it will take, but we need to explore some new options. It will be interesting to watch what happens with "infomercials," which have been used primarily to sell commercial products on TV. They are inexpensive to produce and relatively inexpensive to air. Instead of 30 seconds, the message can be 30 minutes or even 60 minutes long. In addition, the time the show airs can be controlled to some degree because the airtime is paid for, not free. In the meantime, one alternative channel of communication, at least to the youth population, is the music video.

In the recent Musicians for Life campaign on AIDS prevention, which was targeted at minority teens, mainstream television was not the priority. While the campaign did eventually air on all the networks and their affiliated stations, the main focus of distribution was the more than 200 television music video shows, MTV, video jukeboxes, and videos in dance clubs. We were even featured on the video vans that circulate on college campuses and on video screens in record stores, and our public service messages were played during rock concerts, some of which were televised.

Because of the minority youth focus of the campaign, we used some Spanish-speaking recording artists and translated all materials into Spanish. The Spanish-language stations gave the campaign a lot of airtime.

How could present health communication campaign models be improved to make them useful for planning, implementing, and evaluating mass media campaigns?

Communication theorists generally do not understand the creative process involved in producing a public service campaign and do not have a good grasp on how the entertainment industry actually operates. Because of this, as a campaign designer I am often frustrated by their studies and articles.

What roles can formative or summative evaluation play in the relative success of a health communication campaign?

Formative evaluation is one of the most important elements of a campaign. Such evaluation is not always used as much as it should be. It is very important to know who a campaign is supposed to reach while the campaign is being designed. For example, the Musicians for Life AIDS prevention campaign was aimed at teenagers, but it proved very difficult to get the audience data required to shape the campaign. Finally, much valuable information was obtained from focus group studies in California and in Seattle, and from other data collected from federal agencies and from AIDS services organizations. From all these sources, a portrait of the target audience for the campaign was produced, which had a strong impact on the shape of the campaign.

One problem with summative evaluation is that it is very expensive. Public communication campaigns have limited funds and production is so expensive that there is seldom money left over for postcampaign evaluation. However, such evaluations, if done properly, can be important for designing future campaigns.

What are the unique characteristics and special difficulties of preventive health communication campaigns, especially those aimed at high-risk youth?

High-risk youth are difficult to reach with any kind of message, and prevention messages are perhaps the most challenging. A problem of almost all such campaigns is that the organizations involved focus on very narrow topic areas. Examples are the prevention of teenage pregnancy, tobacco use, crack, AIDS, or alcohol abuse. These campaigns are conducted as if the target audiences for the campaigns are all very different. In reality, we are trying to reach the same people with each of these campaigns. The same teenager is going to run away, drop out of school, or abuse alcohol or other drugs. It is a waste of resources when all these groups are fighting for the same television time to reach the same teenagers. These organizations would be more effective if they worked together in a coordinated manner to produce campaigns that address the common denominators.

How do factors such as age groupings, fear appeals, audience segmentation, and use of opinion leaders contribute to the design of mass media campaigns targeted to high-risk youth?

All of those factors contribute to any kind of campaign. Age is certainly a major aspect to consider. To me, the most important group for prevention messages is elementary school children, as preventive health habits can be inculcated more easily in this age group and can have a lasting impact. Audience segmentation strategies are important, but from a practical viewpoint it is difficult to achieve really precise segmentation when messages are aired on television. Therefore campaigns directed at children or other target audiences can only be approximately segmented, for instance, by knowing when children are most likely to watch TV.

It is a problem these days to find role models who are untainted by scandal. It is even more difficult to find role models who will likely remain trouble free. There are not many people who teenagers respect and look up to as heroes, and sometimes these people's images are in conflict with the desired health message. Thus, the chances for success with campaigns using celebrity role models are becoming more limited.

Teenagers are not concerned with long-term health effects. They are more concerned about short-term and immediate effects. They worry about bad breath or yellow fingers from smoking rather than about lung cancer at the age of 50. We have to keep in mind what they care about and what they are concerned about, things like peer approval and body image.

A problem with drug abuse prevention messages is that we are telling people what *not* to do, but not telling them what *to* do. Campaigns are more effective when we tell people what to do. For example, we can tell people to avoid AIDS by using condoms, or to prevent serious injuries by using seat belts in cars.

A more fundamental problem is the social-structural environment of high-risk youth. These young people may have nothing to do. They often do not have recreation facilities such as parks or libraries. There are few programs to tap their energies, and no fun places to go after school. This problem of "nothing to do" affects all the problems that kids have. Instead of saying "Don't have sex," "Don't do crack," or "Don't drink and drive," we should find ways of giving kids something to do.

Publications for teens are not properly exploited by campaigns; there are still untapped ways and means of getting a message across through the teenage print media, for example, by trying to get the right kind of features and news stories printed in the magazines read by teenagers, and putting the right kinds of messages in magazine articles or asking the right kind of questions in interviews with celebrities. Radio can be effective, but the industry is not broadcasting many public service messages these days. We need to find ways to make the music industry and radio more responsive to health issues.

We learn many behaviors from the mass media, such as what to wear, what to eat and drink, and how to behave in certain situations. For instance, seat belt use in television shows has reinforced their use by the audience.

What is the most successful mass media campaign to change health behavior you have known, and why do you think it worked?

I think the antitobacco campaign in the United States has been the most successful recent mass media campaign. It started in the early 1960s, and has been going on since then in various forms. Smokers' insurance premiums were affected, and legislation was passed. Smoking went from being sexy to being offensive. In the 1970s there was a movement in schools to teach very young children about the dangers of using tobacco, with some media supplements, and this strategy seems to have been very effective.

What role should federal, state, or local governments play in media campaigns?

The federal government may in the future need to rely less on established groups such as the Advertising Council for mounting campaigns, and look to other types of organizations with different types of resources to provide campaign messages. To do this the current system for awarding contracts for campaign and message development may also need to be reviewed, to be sure that those best able to access the new media outlets are able to participate in the system.

What organizations and organizational factors contribute to the success or failure of media campaigns?

If one is trying to launch a national campaign, a lot of money and long-term planning are required as well as careful coordination of a number of organizational interests. For limited-budget campaigns to be effective, the target audience has to be defined in a narrow geographical area, a narrow age group, or some other restrictive definition, or any opportunity for impact will be lost.

Turf battles among the different organizations involved in coproducing a campaign are destructive. Production of a media campaign is often easier when control rests with a single authority. Television programming content is produced by consensus in order not to offend anybody, which results in bland programs. PSAs made by committee tend to be forgettable.

New alliances among organizations must be found. For instance, we should involve nonprofit organizations in creating positive productions for television. We must find ways to finance the production of films like *Stand and Deliver*, which cost only about $1 million. This movie was much more effective in keeping kids in school than 10 PSAs saying "Stay in school." Money put into the movie was utilized much more effectively, and contributed to better results. We could make movies on health themes for video, and place them in video stores. This can be done at a much cheaper price than producing PSAs.

What methods would you suggest for financing media campaigns for health?

To begin with, the cost of a PSA campaign, considering its limitations in length and airtime, is excessive. I don't mean to imply that the costs aren't real; they are. I just think we have to find ways to get more for our dollar. We have to explore new ways of creating and getting to the public messages of social importance; we need to investigate new forums. The cost of a few 30-second commercials can be more than that of a low-budget feature film.

As for funding sources, we might think of encouraging nonprofit organizations and government agencies to work together, to pool their funds. Too often agencies are competing for the same audience with the same message and for the same airtime. This is a waste of resources.

The drawbacks to what I've just proposed are that good campaigns are not created by committee and that the federal government and nonprofit organizations are generally not in the vanguard of creative new ventures. Perhaps the government could partner with institutions in a better position to take chances or to produce a potentially controversial message. The government could provide funding but otherwise act in an advisory role. The pooling of funds with nongovernment organizations might also allow for the purchase of airtime, such as the "infomercial" format.

I would like to see a meeting organized, to include representatives of government, television, and the film community; the purpose of which would be to discuss what social messages might look like in the future. If we are to improve on what we are doing now, this can be accomplished only with everyone working together. The current system suits the networks' needs and formats, but they have become outdated for funding organizations.

LAWRENCE KINCAID
Johns Hopkins University

ABOUT THE INTERVIEWEE

Lawrence Kincaid is an Associate Professor in the Division of Behavioral Sciences and Health Education, Department of Health Policy and Management, and a Senior Research Officer for the Center for Communication Programs at Johns Hopkins University. He has more than 15 years' experience in conducting research on communication in Asia and the Near East, Latin America, and Africa. His research on the use of communication to promote family planning and rural development in Korea and in the Philippines led to a new approach to rural development, based on informal communication networks, social support, and local opinion leaders. This approach was featured in *Communication Networks: Toward a New*

Paradigm for Research (Free Press, 1981), which Kincaid coauthored with Everett Rogers. This experience illuminated many important differences in the practice of communication in the East compared with the West. These differences also were highlighted in the first major edited book on this subject, *Communication Theory: Eastern and Western Perspectives* (Academic Press, 1987), which Kincaid edited.

Dr. Kincaid earned his B.A. degree in psychology from the University of Kansas, and his M.A. and Ph.D. in communication from Michigan State University. He taught and conducted research in communication for the East-West Center at the University of Hawaii for 10 years and at the State University of New York at Albany for 4 years. He has been at Johns Hopkins University since 1987.

Dr. Kincaid has been involved in many campaigns in the Third World, including some directed at youth, although not specifically for drug abuse prevention. At present, he is primarily involved with evaluating family planning communication campaigns.

* * *

What are the most common reasons mass media campaigns do not achieve their hoped-for results, and what are the most common reasons some campaigns are relatively successful?

Campaigns fail largely for not saying the right thing to the right audience. Formative research is not done, and audience characteristics are not known. Precampaign interaction with the audience is absolutely essential, but this is not necessarily best done through a survey questionnaire; interpersonal contact methods are much more powerful. Also, the choice of the right media to use for a particular audience is important. Finally, some convergence between the audience and the designers is required to stimulate the best and most productive creative content for campaign messages.

How could present health communication campaign models be improved to make them useful for planning, implementing, and evaluating mass media campaigns?

Theoretical models of public communication are generally given lip service by campaign designers, but are not actually utilized in the day-to-day work of creating or running a campaign. Many issues have not yet been well addressed by any of the available theories. For instance, theories currently do not discuss how to achieve a better balance between the cognitive and the emotional contents of a campaign message.

What roles can formative or summative evaluation play in the relative success of a health communication campaign?

Summative evaluation is seldom utilized properly. As a result, the knowledge that may be derived from an evaluation is not recycled back into the design of future campaigns. Summative evaluation is used mainly for obtaining future funds (to continue a current campaign or begin a new one) by showing whether some particular approach was effective or not. While this isn't inappropriate, it doesn't usually lead to an increase in overall knowledge or skill levels about campaigns.

What are the unique characteristics and special difficulties of preventive health communication campaigns, especially those aimed at high-risk youth?

One prominent characteristic of youth is that they are at a stage in life where they are defining themselves, and thus are dependent on others, especially their peers, in this defining process. Moreover, many powerful biological changes are taking place and this influences behavior, sometimes in dramatic ways. Campaigns need to be designed to reflect both interpersonal and intrapersonal variables of this sort. Furthermore, there are significant differences within the overall population of "high-risk youth" that must be taken into account. For instance, in a recent study correlating behavioral, social, and biological variables, testosterone levels explained more than 50% of the variance for males, but in females, hormone levels did not explain much variance. For females, social variables explained much more variance in behavior.

How do factors such as age groupings, fear appeals, audience segmentation, and use of opinion leaders contribute to the design of mass media campaigns targeted to high-risk youth?

Strong fear appeals are not effective. Fear appeals should be moderate, should be combined with positive themes, and should serve only as a reminder of negative consequences.

Any mass medium can be successful in health campaigns, if used effectively, as determined by formative research. Multiple communication media should be used in most campaigns. In some cases, we have made artificial separations in our conceptualization of the media. For instance, the portrayal of interpersonal interaction in a film, where audience members participate vicariously in the interpersonal interaction being shown, is in one way actually interpersonal communication, not mass communication. Effectiveness depends on how well the portrayal of that interpersonal interaction is done.

What role should federal, state, or local governments play in media campaigns?

In the United States, private and voluntary agencies are strong. The role of the government should be to get these agencies started in designing and operating campaigns by offering seed money. An even more important function of the government can be to create a *societal* structure through legal and policy decisions that makes it easier for mass media health campaigns to succeed. An example is banning smoking in public places, in turn supporting antismoking campaigns.

What organizations and organizational factors contribute to the success or failure of media campaigns?

Usually in organizations associated with a mass media health campaign only a *part* of the organization is aware of, or involved with, the campaign. Typically, there is a need to involve the entire organization in a campaign, especially the top leadership. Also, *networking* among the various organizations involved in a campaign is important, to permit sharing of resources, problem solving, and so forth.

What methods would you suggest for financing media campaigns for health?

To increase the financial viability of a campaign, a strategy should be built into the system whereby there is a sale of some media products at the "end of the line" for the campaign's activities. This is a motivation for those who are actually involved in the implementation, and at the same time keeps the campaign financially sound.

DAVID McCALLUM
Center for Risk Communication

ABOUT THE INTERVIEWEE

David McCallum is Deputy Director of the Center for Risk Communication of Columbia University and is Director of its Washington,

D.C., program. Previously, he founded and directed the Program o
Risk Communication at Georgetown University Medical Center. He i
primarily involved in research analysis, consultation, and disseminatio
efforts aimed at understanding the flow of information on consumer an
environmental health issues among scientists, practitioners, journalists
and consumers.

Dr. McCallum was formerly a Senior Analyst in the U.S. Congres
Office of Technology Assessment. He also coordinated technolog
transfer activities at the National Heart, Lung, and Blood Institute, an
served as Director of Chronic Disease Control for the State of Sout
Carolina. He has also directed research and development for Procte
and Gamble, Inc., and has served in many government and privat
agency posts examining technology assessment and transfer, diseas
prevention, and public health.

Dr. McCallum received a B.S. in chemical engineering from Nort
Carolina State University and an M.S. in chemical engineering an
Ph.D. in biomedical engineering from the University of Virginia. H
has been involved in designing and consulting on mass media healt
campaigns on a variety of issues, mostly having to do with communi
cation of health risks.

* * *

*What are the most common reasons mass media campaigns do no
achieve their hoped-for results, and what are the most common reason.
some campaigns are relatively successful?*

The chief problem limiting campaign success is that the objective
are simply not clear. Without clear objectives, a campaign loses focu
and it becomes difficult to measure its achievements. Moreover, man
campaign designs do not integrate information and skills acquisitio
with behavioral incentives and barriers, so that the design does not dea
with the full spectrum of relevant variables that relate to stimulating
knowledge, attitude, or behavior change. Also, some campaigns ma
just create awareness and a certain level of cognitive dissonance, bu
are not constructed to provide a means for resolving the dissonance the
create. Campaign designers also may limit campaigns' effectiveness i
they do not recognize the need to address *secondary audiences*, such a
health professionals in the clinics where those affected by the campaig
will come to obtain services the campaign teaches them about.

There should be a combination of creativity and enthusiasm in the campaign's messages, to make them as impactful as possible. The messages should provide strong *incentives* to support the changed behavior, and should support *risk taking* or experimenting with new ideas. In order to understand what incentives exist or what risk taking means for a particular audience, formative research is needed; but this often does not happen. Even communications professionals assume audience characteristics many times.

The timing of a media campaign is one of the most important factors in its success. Timing can be thought of as the confluence of all the campaign variables coming together, including how the particular health issue is positioned politically. Methods for assessing the conditions that make up "campaign timing" include monitoring of national polls, checking data bases in the particular health issue area for emerging trends, looking at what the mass media are saying about the issues, surveying or interviewing people, and sometimes reading between the lines in interpreting social trends based upon all the preceding sources.

How could present health communication campaign models be improved to make them useful for planning, implementing, and evaluating mass media campaigns?

All campaign models basically are conceptually very similar. However, by the time these models become useful for "real-time" campaign design, they also become cumbersome to handle. Thus models are, and will remain, inadequate for the conduct of campaigns. Also, many models may have something to offer; we should not become obsessed with just one model.

One danger in theories based upon modeling concepts is that the assumptions limiting the correspondence between the model and the real world are often not stated. This can lead to inappropriate use of the model in designing a campaign.

We must understand the natural processes taking place in people's response to a campaign, through observation and evaluation, and this information should be "put back into" the model in terms of refining it and improving it—or at some point throwing the model away if it just doesn't seem to correspond to reality.

What roles can formative or summative evaluation play in the relative success of a health communication campaign?

Outcome evaluation should be done only if it can be done comprehensively, so that the whole array of variables relevant to a campaign can be measured. Most of the time, the will and the resources to do this just aren't there. The focus of outcome evaluation should be to prove that a particular *strategy* or set of strategies used in a campaign can be successful (as opposed to showing that the *campaign* was successful, which is much less useful for building knowledge for future campaigns).

What are the unique characteristics and special difficulties of preventive health communication campaigns, especially those aimed at high-risk youth?

It is difficult to show high-risk youth that there is something in the messages of most mass media health campaigns for them. Youth in general are "high denial," and high-risk youth (who are also usually from economically deprived families) have low levels of hope about their futures. Thus prevention-oriented campaigns have only limited effects. The real causes of drug abuse lie in social factors, and without intervening at these levels, the chances for change are limited. Also, youth have the feeling of being invulnerable and it is difficult to break through this, either through a campaign or in real life. For example, research shows that in order for them to adopt AIDS prevention behavior, youth need to have *two* friends die from AIDS (not just one).

How do factors such as age groupings, fear appeals, audience segmentation, and use of opinion leaders contribute to the design of mass media campaigns targeted to high-risk youth?

Major transition points in the lives of youth are the ages at which a campaign typically should concentrate—entering middle school, taking a job, etc. These are the life stages at which there may be more openness to considering health-related information and even possible behavior change.

Fear appeals can be effective in a health campaign if an appropriate *outlet* for the fear is then provided as part of the campaign activities. In general, we should be very careful when using fear appeals because they often have negative outcomes. Youth generally are motivated by two incentives: economic success and social acceptance. Campaigns that trade on these two incentives are more likely to be successful.

Audience segmentation depends on the particulars of message content. High degrees of segmentation are not usually necessary to have a significant campaign, but an optimum should be found.

Opinion leaders can be discovered through formative evaluation. Also, the preference of the target audience for particular types of role models can be determined through this process. Involvement of opinion leaders can be motivated by appealing to their egos and by using methods designed to enhance their prestige as a result of campaign participation.

Mass and interpersonal communication methods are highly intertwined and are much more circular than the classic two-step flow model implies. Messages flowing through the mass media reflect social norms, but also help to create them. Maximum campaign success is achieved when the same basic message is flowing in both the mass and interpersonal communication channels, and this requires very careful coordination and effort.

What is the most successful mass media campaign to change health behavior you have known, and why do you think it worked?

A national campaign to reduce high blood pressure was very successful, in part, because of its corporate backing. This campaign provided an opportunity for drug companies to make money by selling drugs for high blood pressure, which is not necessarily undesirable as long as the campaign objectives are also met. A linkage between health and economic objectives often can be a big factor in a campaign's success. Private sector companies are simply more likely to get involved in areas where financial rewards are possible. However, this is not even possible for all campaign areas. For example, high-risk youth do not have economic clout, and thus are in a weak position to command attention from advertisers of health-oriented products.

What role should federal, state, or local governments play in media campaigns?

The government's role in communication campaigns concerns primarily the *efficiency* and *effectiveness* of campaigns. The federal government plays a major role in national agenda-setting for an issue, and in creating basic awareness about it. The federal government can bring delicate issues out into the open, and can provide leadership on an issue that local government typically cannot. However, local or state governments, knowing local conditions, also can help promote overall effectiveness of a media campaign.

What organizations and organizational factors contribute to the success or failure of media campaigns?

Negotiation skills to resolve conflicts are an asset any organization should have for becoming involved in media campaigns. Most health topics involve some controversy, and organizations that cannot productively face and resolve such controversy run a high risk of failure for the mass media campaign.

In dealing with media organizations such as television or radio groups, we must not have overly high expectations from the mass media organizations, and we must recognize that the media have their own agenda, and we have to adjust our agenda to theirs. They control the airtime, so this compromise really is necessary even when the topic is of urgent importance.

Advocacy groups are effective for creating awareness in a media campaign, but not good at linking to any kind of strategic campaign activity, as they can create a great deal of controversy and thus jeopardize the campaign's success in a particular setting. Also, for any organization, the dangers of failure are so much more devastating than the rewards for success that campaign designers and those supporting them in organizations tend to be overly conservative.

What methods would you suggest for financing media campaigns for health?

Corporate sponsorship has not been fully tapped yet for public campaigns as a means of financing. Many campaigns could certainly benefit from the additional resources such private sector involvement would bring.

JACQUELINE E. McDONALD
Scott Newman Center

ABOUT THE INTERVIEWEE

Jacqueline E. McDonald is the President of the Scott Newman Center in Los Angeles and directs the day-to-day operations of this drug prevention/education organization. The center seeks to use media creatively in developing substance abuse prevention materials for young people, parents, and the community.

Since McDonald began working with the organization in 1985, the center has produced two films: a junior high school drug prevention film, *Straight at Ya,* funded by the U.S. Department of Education for nationwide distribution; and *Drug Free Kids: A Parents' Guide,* a 70-minute home video that has been shown nationally on PBS.

Recent drug prevention projects developed by the center include Neighborhoods in Action, a community outreach program that has been implemented in 13 states; and the PSA (Prevent Substance Abuse) project for high school students, implemented in 18 states.

One of the center's current projects is All Babies Count, a joint venture with the Washington-based organization Very Special Arts. All Babies Count seeks to implement a national media campaign to promote awareness of the problem and support for infants at risk for drug abuse (through maternal drug use) and their families among the general public, and to provide information and education for specific target audiences, such as women of childbearing age. (The two organizations brought together representatives from six different disciplines—business and industry, community-based organizations, education, health professionals, media, and public policy—for a two-day strategy session to elicit common concerns and goals before beginning to plan the campaign. Certainly, considering the current statistics on teenage pregnancy, much of the campaign will be targeted to high-risk youth.)

Prior to joining the Scott Newman Center, Ms. McDonald taught English and special programs in both the Los Angeles and Ventura Unified school districts and worked in the entertainment industry as a literary agent and in management for health promotion organizations. She earned a B.A. from Northwestern University and a master's degree in education from California State University at Northridge.

Ms. McDonald currently serves on three committees of the California State Department of Education: the AIDS/HIV Advisory Committee; the Superintendent's Drug, Alcohol and Tobacco Advisory Committee; and the Human Genetics & Birth Defects Prevention Education Program Task Force. She is also a member of the Office for Substance Abuse Prevention's ad hoc task force on public and private sector initiatives.

* * *

What are the most common reasons mass media campaigns do not achieve their hoped-for results, and what are the most common reasons some campaigns are relatively successful?

Many mass media campaigns are ineffective because they are boring and do not capture the interest of the intended target audience, particularly when the target audience is youth. Sometimes the target audience is not identified specifically enough. Even after precise identification, strategies for reaching a specific target audience with an appropriate message are not researched carefully enough, which can result in a very broad—and thus weak—message. Youth are inundated with creative messages in many media, all of which are intended to sell products of all kinds. To get "over and through" these powerful messages and their distractions (and sometimes countermessages, as with alcohol and cigarette ads), we have to be equally creative to hold the attention of youth with antidrug messages.

Successful campaigns thoroughly research the target audience, utilize strategies that are known to appeal to that target audience, and use a number of media avenues (e.g., television, radio, print, billboards) to call attention to the same basic message. They are also *long-term campaigns*, which recognize that attitude and behavior changes do not take place quickly.

How could present health communication campaign models be improved to make them useful for planning, implementing, and evaluating mass media campaigns?

A greater emphasis on researching *all* aspects of the target audience during the planning stages of a public health campaign would ensure greater effectiveness. Careful planning of the dissemination routes needed in order to secure the greatest exposure for the message among the identified target audience would also be helpful.

What roles can formative or summative evaluation play in the relative success of a health communication campaign?

Formative evaluation plays a crucial part in the success of any campaign. Not only does it provide a testing ground to make sure the messages used are appropriate for the target audience, it also offers a vehicle for getting the proposed target audience to "buy into" the campaign in the first place.

What are the unique characteristics and special difficulties of preventive health communication campaigns, especially those aimed at high-risk youth?

High-risk youth probably constitute the most difficult target audience to reach with a mass media campaign. These young people are not usually readers or "pamphlet pickers." They therefore don't use some of the cheapest and most readily available media, such as newspapers. Moreover, it would be very difficult for even the most carefully thought-out antidrug mass media campaign to address all the surrounding issues of poverty, joblessness, lack of role models, and so on that promote the use of alcohol and other drugs among high-risk youth. It's not good enough to ask a specific group to cease high-risk behavior that is an unfortunate part of their environment without offering alternatives. Therefore, the responsibility for helping to create the social change needed to reduce the temptation to use drugs is there—this is clearly the long-term path.

How do factors such as age groupings, fear appeals, audience segmentation, and use of opinion leaders contribute to the design of mass media campaigns targeted to high-risk youth?

We need to start teaching youth about drugs and other health-related issues at a much younger age than has been conventional up to now. To start teaching prevention in junior high school is much too late for high-risk youth, who typically have a significant high school dropout rate. Rather than dwelling specifically on drug abuse issues with younger children, promoting a more general awareness of broader health concerns might be more effective. This approach also could be designed to promote self-esteem among target high-risk youth.

Fear appeals do not seem to work well with most young people; fear of death is too far away from them. For example, the message that you should stop smoking because you will die at 65 years of age rather than 75 has little meaning for someone aged 16. Reports from those working with inner-city youth say that as everyday violence increases, attitudes about death and dying have become increasingly fatalistic. This also reduces any relation to reality of a message about threat of dying.

Audience segmentation strategies are extremely important for reaching high-risk youth effectively. Not to identify as narrowly as possible the primary audiences the campaign is intended to influence runs the risk of creating so broad a message, it reaches *no one* effectively!

It is extremely important to identify and cultivate opinion leaders in high-risk communities. Probably not enough emphasis is placed on this strategy in many campaigns, and there is limited understanding among campaign designers about how to do it. Well-intentioned mass media campaigns planned by outsiders are often unwelcome in the targeted communities, and may even be rejected because respected community members were not brought into the planning process early on.

Incentives, badges, ribbons, stars, and other physical incentives probably work best with younger children. Incentives such as scholarships have worked with older students, especially when combined with other strategies such as mentoring by a specific group in the community. For young people, it is important to stress positive attributes, such as increased popularity and peer approval, for ceasing or acquiring a particular health-related behavior.

For junior high and high school students, radio could be an effective channel. In most campaigns, radio has not yet been used as much as it could be. Also, initiating courses in media literacy could become a tool for preventing the use of alcohol and other drugs. Most young people are totally unaware of the fact that they are the target audience not only for jeans and shoe manufacturers, but also too often for the manufacturers of alcohol and tobacco, products well researched as the precursors for young people to heavier drug use. Learning how to be more effective consumers of media can help youth to turn off pro-use messages.

The most effective mass-interpersonal communication relationship occurs when the media campaign successfully motivates people to think about and discuss a specific issue. Enlisting respected opinion leaders to promote discussion of the issue can be a useful strategy for that purpose.

Audience bombardment is the key to a successful media campaign. This means using all media avenues available over an extended period of time, and coordinating the various channels in as many ways as possible.

What is the most successful mass media campaign to change health behavior you have known, and why do you think it worked?

Probably the antismoking campaign of the 1960s has been the most impactful mass media campaign to date. The impact of the surgeon general's report in 1964, followed by the media campaign, really focused the public's attention on this issue. The result has been a significant decline in smoking among most groups, and a change in the overall social perception of smoking.

What role should federal, state, or local governments play in media campaigns?

Government at all levels can play successful roles in media campaigns, especially when government agencies work closely with private sector people and organizations familiar with the designated target audience. For example, the state of California staged a mass media antismoking campaign that was creative and effective for the most part and included tie-ins with many local, grass-roots organizations. Government agencies often have the necessary funds to undertake and maintain a successful campaign, whereas such resources may not be so readily available to private agencies—but they can participate in a campaign's success in many other ways.

What organizations and organizational factors contribute to the success or failure of media campaigns?

The Harvard Alcohol Project utilized the television networks most successfully in its designated driver campaign, by holding small seminars with personnel of popular TV series to explain and discuss this issue. Using the designated driver idea in various prime-time television show segments clearly enhanced other aspects of the overall Don't Drink and Drive campaign the project coordinated.

The formation of the Ad Council enabled a greater number of creative PSAs and print messages on health and social issues to be produced than if a single agency had undertaken the same sets of tasks on drug abuse and other issues. In addition, the Ad Council-produced messages clearly had wider dissemination than those produced by a single ad agency.

What methods would you suggest for financing media campaigns for health?

As it becomes increasingly evident to employers that preventing illness of all kinds is indeed cost-effective, *business and industry* may become a new resource for funding media campaigns for health issues. Tie-ins with funding sources in the public sector might also be possible, as has happened in a number of health service areas recently.

JOHN V. PAVLIK
Freedom Forum Media Studies Center

ABOUT THE INTERVIEWEE

John V. Pavlik is Associate Director for Research and Technology Studies, Freedom Forum Media Studies Center, Columbia University. He was formerly Assistant Professor and Graduate Studies Director in the School of Communications, Pennsylvania State University. He is the author of numerous scholarly publications, ranging from research articles on health communication to public relations campaign planning. He is the author of *Public Relations: What Research Tells Us*. He has also authored computer software for public relations planning and management and for journalism and mass communication education. A former public relations officer, Pavlik has served as a research consultant to a number of organizations. His Ph.D. in mass communication is from the University of Minnesota, where he wrote his dissertation on the Minnesota Heart Health Program.

Dr. Pavlik has been primarily involved as a campaign designer with the media aspects of the multidisciplinary Minnesota Heart Health Program. The target audience of this program was adults ages 25 to 74.

*   *   *

What are the most common reasons mass media campaigns do not achieve their hoped-for results, and what are the most common reasons some campaigns are relatively successful?

Two classic studies illustrate the background for studying the effects of mass media campaigns. The first is by Herbert M. Hyman and Paul Sheatsley, "Some Reasons Why Information Campaigns Fail," published in *Public Opinion Quarterly* in 1947. These researchers found that media campaigns failed largely because of both physical barriers and psychological barriers to using the information presented. In particular, they found that campaign messages were interpreted by individuals according to their *predispositions* and existing schemas for thinking. The barrier of "selective perception" is still important in understanding diminishing campaign efforts. Other psychological variables, such as degree of involvement and self-efficacy, also determine how a campaign message is received by an individual.

The second study is by Harold Mendelsohn, "Some Reasons Why Information Campaigns Can Succeed," published in 1973 in *Public Opinion Quarterly.* This piece essentially turns Hyman and Sheatsley's argument around. Mendelsohn suggests ways in which campaigns can be successful: (1) by determining and identifying their appropriate target audience, (2) by identifying the appropriate messages and appeals to be used, (3) by identifying the right media to be used with the given audience, and (4) by using interpersonal channels to reach the target audience. The Minnesota Heart Health Program was a success because it utilized these observations to find appropriate media channels (such as direct mail), developed the right message appeals, mobilized community support, and used the media in conjunction with local health screening centers.

Some campaigns fail by not reaching the intended audience. Another problem lies in the measurement of behavior change, which is usually measured by average scores. But change may not always be reflected by averages!

Also, the campaign effort may not be done well enough or may not be strong enough to have an effect. In addition, general trends in society may affect campaigns. A social problem that is already moving in the desired direction—for example, reduction of risk factors for heart disease—can confound the measurement of campaign effects. An improved study design of impacts is possible if a subgroup of the population that is at high risk is identified that does *not* have a natural trend to solving whatever the health problem is. Unfortunately, the pattern of most mass media is to avoid high-risk subgroups and concentrate instead on mainstream society, where the messages are typically not very relevant.

Campaigns succeed by identifying audiences, using knowledge of information processing effectively, and selecting media vehicles precisely. Successful campaigns utilize an interdisciplinary approach, combining expertise and knowledge from mass communication, medicine, and public health, among other topical areas. Successful campaigns are more holistic and comprehensive, and have longer-term perspectives, than do less successful ones. Commitment over time is important if a campaign is to succeed.

How could present health communication campaign models be improved to make them useful for planning, implementing, and evaluating mass media campaigns?

The theoretical models of communication campaigns are generally adequate for usefulness in designing and implementing campaigns. The multicultural characteristics of audiences are important. Targeting a campaign to the Native American population would be extremely useful, as this population has many social problems not yet fully addressed, such as alcoholism. But existing models do not take into account cultural differences among subaudiences for a mass media health campaign.

A campaign needs to have a strong theoretical basis, along with a conceptual basis for understanding the audience, in order to succeed. Educational messages are now placed within television programming by involving TV and movie producers and scriptwriters in health campaigns. In coming years, this entertainment-education strategy will be very important, as the Harvard Alcohol Project suggests.

What roles can formative or summative evaluation play in the relative success of a health communication campaign?

Much has been learned about the role of formative research in message formulation and media selection. Focus groups and quasi-experimental studies are sometimes used to study effects of different message strategies. Summative research is generally required by funding agencies, which want to see hard data concerning reduction in the audience of risk factors or in morbidity and mortality, and changes in attitudes, beliefs, and behavior patterns.

How do factors such as age groupings, fear appeals, audience segmentation, and use of opinion leaders contribute to the design of mass media campaigns targeted to high-risk youth?

The age group of junior high school to high school is most suitable for campaign targeting, because this is the point when children start making decisions about their own lives. Very creative approaches are required to reach an audience of children and youth through media channels. A looming problem is the increasing rate of AIDS among teenagers in the United States, however, so that there really isn't a choice about learning how to do the best we can.

Fear appeals produce an effect, but it may not be the campaign effect that is desired! Fear appeals can arouse emotional reactions, but whether they are effective in changing behavior in the desired direction is not clear. Moderate appeals are more effective, as they do not as easily arouse psychological defense mechanisms. Children and youth, who believe they are immortal, are especially likely to have defensive or denial reactions.

Audience segmentation strategies are critical and quite fundamental to the process of effective mass media campaigns. After specific audiences are identified, appropriate messages must be designed to reach them through appropriate media vehicles. All these factors are really critical to campaign success.

Opinion leaders may be important to youth, but identifying such leaders may be difficult. Also, there is much we don't know about these influential people as they relate to mass media health campaigns. For instance, are opinion leaders for youth cross-situational or situation specific?

Youth are often very short-term oriented, so trying to make them respond to messages about long-term benefits of preventive health behaviors may not be effective. We must use short-term, immediate rewards to motivate youth. We should highlight the *social* consequences of their health-related actions, such as becoming more or less popular, or being more accepted or ignored by their peers. Interpersonal communication in peer groups is very influential in shaping the perceptions and decisions of youth on these matters, so any way we can intervene with that process of interpersonal sharing may be particularly fruitful.

Music on television and radio, and also recorded music, is an effective channel for reaching youth. We also need to look at special kinds of television programming, such as MTV; at high-technology-oriented activities, such as computer and telephone use; and at interpersonal communication strategies, such as clubs and meetings, as potential channels for reaching youth.

Frequency of exposure is very important. It can be achieved with music, especially via radio. Younger children have different media habits from their older peers, and we should keep this fact in mind during campaign design. For instance, print media generally are difficult to use with children and youth, except perhaps comic books, pamphlets, or posters.

What was the most successful mass media campaign to change health behavior you have known, and why do you think it worked?

The Minnesota Heart Disease Prevention Project was highly successful. Other successful campaigns include the heart disease prevention projects at Stanford, Pawtucket (Rhode Island), and North Karelia (in Finland). These projects utilized a multidisciplinary, holistic approach to "selling the message" they had to offer, and all of them included a substantial evaluation component.

What role should federal, state, or local governments play in media campaigns?

The government provides funding, and so it has a role to play in health campaigns. A positive factor of government's involvement is that it requires *accountability* from the people executing the campaign. The government should not be involved in the theoretical and creative development of the campaign. It is best involved in the accountability component, and in ensuring that the information generated by campaign evaluation is shared widely so that future campaigns can be improved. Local government personnel are often opinion leaders and power brokers in their communities, and so hold much influence over institutions; thus the participation of local government in any mass media health campaign is very important.

What methods would you suggest for financing media campaigns for health?

A major problem with the media has been that PSA airtimes are allocated when the target audience is not watching. If the media contribute quality time, or make available for purchase such time at lowered rates, that would be helpful. Media costs are one of the major expenses of a campaign.

MARY ANN PENTZ
University of Southern California

ABOUT THE INTERVIEWEE

Mary Ann Pentz is Associate Professor of Research, Director of Community Prevention Research, and Chair of Graduate Studies for the Institute for Health Promotion and Disease Prevention Research, Department of Preventive Medicine, University of Southern California.

Prior to coming to USC in 1983, she was Assistant Professor in the Psychology Department at the University of Tennessee in Knoxville.

Dr. Pentz has served as principal investigator on a number of research projects, including a project on stress prevention in early adolescence for the National Institute of Mental Health and a comprehensive community drug abuse prevention program for the National Institute on Drug Abuse. Her research experience has included studies of self-efficacy and social skills training for adolescents, adolescent health promotion through stress and drug use prevention, school-based consultation for reduction of mal-adaptation in youth, and community approaches to health promotion and disease prevention in youth (school, family, media, and community organization intervention research).

Dr. Pentz received a B.A. from Hamilton College (Clinton, New York) in 1972, and an M.A. and Ph.D. from Syracuse University in 1976 and 1978, respectively. She has been widely published in a number of professional journals, including the *Journal of School Health, American Journal of Epidemiology,* and *Journal of the American Medical Association,* and is the author of a number of book chapters, including "Social Competence and Self-Efficacy as Determinants of Substance Use in Adolescents," in T. A. Wills and S. Shiffman (Eds.), *Coping and Substance Use* (Academic Press, 1985).

Dr. Pentz has been involved in mass media campaigns for drug abuse prevention with adolescent youth (including high-risk youth) as part of her research program concerning the Kansas City and Indianapolis substance abuse prevention campaigns. Each campaign has five components—a school program, a parent program, community organization with city leaders, health policy change, and mass media programming. The mass media campaigns have involved paid commercials, news series on television and radio, PSAs, print articles and editorials, newsletters, and radio and television talk shows.

* * *

What are the most common reasons mass media campaigns do not achieve their hoped-for results, and what are the most common reasons some campaigns are relatively successful?

Many campaigns fail because of their short-term duration, broad scope, and insufficient targeting for specific high-risk audiences. Media campaigns can achieve knowledge and motivational change, and some attitude change, but they are not geared to enough longevity to change overt behavior.

Mass media campaigns can be relatively successful if the outcomes are defined as different from behavior change per se, or are defined as a different kind of behavior. For example, campaigns may be quite successful that are aimed at behavior change of giving donations of money, or making telephone calls—behaviors that are easily understood, and for which a great deal of teaching *or* learning is not required. There have been some campaigns in Australia that actually illustrated the behavior of making a telephone call to a smoking-cessation clinic, and the campaign sent enrollment up in the clinics. Another reason for success depends on who the organizers are and what kind of networking they set up initially. For example, in the Kansas City project there was a very good system of interpersonal communication first and the leaders who set the ball rolling were respected in the community, which led to a snowballing or diffusion effect.

How could present health communication campaign models be improved to make them useful for planning, implementing, and evaluating mass media campaigns?

Some models are excellent conceptually. One type of model focuses on "microlevel communication," the interpersonal networking through which preventive health ideas diffuse. The second type of campaign model deals with a much broader systems-level analysis of the entire environment in which the campaign operates. A blend of both these conceptual approaches is probably needed to make for the greatest success in understanding how campaigns work.

What roles can formative or summative evaluation play in the relative success of a health communication campaign?

Both formative and summative evaluation are important. Focus groups should be conducted with consumers in the target audience to begin the formative process. From the campaign experts come other initial planning inputs: the logistics and likelihood of mounting a campaign, the costs, and the timing. The focus groups also can help determine whether the content that is planned is acceptable to the people in the mass media who are actual writers and producers.

The target audience analysis reveals what kinds of mass media they normally use, and how long and in how many ways the message can be shown before the people show fatigue. Focus groups can also reveal the likely channel, how a message gets across, if the message is coming across as intended or needs to be reframed, if the design of the campaign is user friendly to the people in the mass media who have to develop the messages, and whether what is proposed by the researchers can be translated easily by campaign implementers into messages.

Summative evaluation is perhaps best done on an annual basis, rather than at the end of a very large project. In the case of our projects in Kansas City and Indianapolis, presentation of annual evaluation study findings is used as a media event, by holding an annual press conference in each city, which also gets picked up by the media. The summative evaluation outcome data on drug use are used as feedback to the project, so that people involved in the campaign know where the project is going.

What are the unique characteristics and special difficulties of preventive health communication campaigns, especially those aimed at high-risk youth?

A potential characteristic of effective health prevention campaigns is that one can focus on positive benefits, especially for youth. Prevention is a difficult concept to work with for the public, policymakers, and professionals in the mass media. It is not easy to see the "results" of prevention because the results are not visible and may be years in coming. It is easier to show (on television) the drug user who went through treatment. It is not easy to show young people who are not yet shooting drugs.

With high-risk youth, the difficulty is that we can run the risk of negative labeling when we portray or convey that it is only a certain type of youth who indulges in such behavior. Somehow, during the campaign, youth get identified as the campaign target by themselves or their friends, and these youth get isolated and alienated.

How do factors such as age groupings, fear appeals, audience segmentation, and use of opinion leaders contribute to the design of mass media campaigns targeted to high-risk youth?

The age group to target depends on the definition of *high risk*. If high risk is defined on the basis of demographics, like low socioeconomic status, minority group membership, unemployed parents, or single heads of household, then a campaign should start at the turning point when the youth start questioning their environment. Youth from disadvantaged groups start waking up to their limited opportunities in late adolescence and the early 20s. This is the age group that we must target.

If we are looking for specific behaviors such as drug use, we should target the age group in the transition time between elementary school and high school. If the risk behavior is eating habits, then we should start in elementary school, because it is at that point that eating habits and exercise patterns are established. For the risk of pregnancy and sexually transmitted diseases, we must start at early adolescence and continue through mid-adolescence.

In drug use prevention, fear appeals generally are not useful. Some fear appeals, however, may motivate parents to seek prevention or treatment programs for their kids.

Audience segmentation is essential. For a general information base, campaign segmentation is not required. A segmentation strategy that has not been tried much is to segment according to the *behavioral context* the targeted person is experiencing (from his or her viewpoint) in terms of risk behavior.

To discover the opinion leaders in Kansas City and Indianapolis, the researchers read background political and business material, newspapers, and policy statements, and found out who were the well-respected business leaders who had a history of public service. They found people who are listened to by the public and who have good track records of having completed activities for the public before. Then they started with a small handful of these leaders and asked them what other people they would nominate, and so on, until over a period of time a consensus of 25-50 people was identified. There are two ways to motivate these opinion leaders: If the message or the campaign that they are being asked to get involved with is for the good of the community, typically that is the motivation, and second, in the case of the two drug prevention projects, the initial set of leaders was requested to call ahead and prepare the ground for meetings and to try to influence the second set of leaders.

The use of incentives and disincentives depends upon the type of risk. If a demographic definition of high risk is followed, then the incentives should be a combination of short-term and long-term alternatives that provide the target audience with better services and economic opportunities than they had before. If high risk is defined by behavior or by disease, then the incentives are more centered on the behavioral contextual situations. The incentive is the hook that is provided for the person in that situation to seek information about behavior change or to take preventive measures.

For adolescents, surprisingly, adults and particularly parents still have much influence over knowledge, attitudes, and behaviors. Respected peers and parents are the two primary communication channels for youth. Highly trained teachers can be very good interpersonal channels, but without training in the particular risk area, they are not effective. Any program channel that provides for direct, hands-on experience has the most effect. The hands-on programming could be provided in schools. For the broadest range of a message, television is effective, for different segments of youth radio is effective, and we should use print only if we are trying to reach a higher socioeconomic category.

Mass media can be used at different stages in prevention campaigns. Before the campaign begins, messages can be broadcast that it will begin shortly. When the campaign is in place, messages are highlighted, and some are targeted to parents. Then, participation in the campaign is reinforced by repeating the messages. Next, the messages present the campaign as an ongoing activity. The mass media have the capacity to make items newsworthy and salient, which spurs interpersonal communication.

The most effective media mix also has to involve the length of the campaign. In any project, we must take care that not too much "noise" is created so that people start blanking out the information if it comes at them continuously. So in the two USC projects, the mass media campaigns are cyclic and are not always "on." Also in these two projects, production teams have developed videotapes that are resources for the project as they get used a number of times for special interest groups, for example, business groups to whom the tapes are shown as promotional materials.

What is the most successful mass media campaign to change health behavior you have known, and why do you think it worked?

Two mass media campaigns that were focused on specific outcomes were relatively successful. Milton Rokeach's work in the Great American Values Test did not achieve behavioral change per se, but the intended effects were observed. The campaign worked because the rest of the programming was blacked out, the program itself was a "fun thing" to do for the audience, as it was an absorbing self-test, and a very credible celebrity introduced it.

A successful campaign also was conducted by Dr. John Pierce in Australia on smoking cessation. His PSAs showed illustrative behavior. Among the longer-term campaigns, the heart disease prevention projects of Stanford and in North Karelia have been relatively successful. However, it is not easy to see the effects of the mass media alone in such projects.

What role should federal, state, or local governments play in media campaigns?

Governments can play key roles in communication campaigns: One is to disseminate information through the mass media about what the local rulings are regarding the issue. Second, they can share information about the resources attached to the issue.

What organizations and organizational factors contribute to the success or failure of media campaigns?

In most media campaigns, there is a great competition among various television and radio stations and newspapers to get the news out first. It is difficult to involve the media on a cohesive basis. Opinion leaders in business, if motivated, can be very helpful to a media campaign over time, and with a trustful relationship, they will begin to seek out the media. Also it is helpful to familiarize media representatives with the theory behind the campaign. This approach is very often overlooked. We should not tell the creative people what to do, but just steer them to what works and away from what does not.

What methods would you suggest for financing media campaigns for health?

A good bit of prime-time television was donated to the two USC projects by virtue of showing to the mass media the benefits of the campaign for the viewing public, and also for the high-powered business and community leaders behind it. Increasingly, the mass media are "building in" some amount of public service issues in their content, and we should be ready to utilize this opportunity. Also, some of the money set aside by the federal government for prevention is being wasted on libraries and videotapes that are never used.

RONALD E. RICE
Rutgers University

ABOUT THE INTERVIEWEE

Ronald E. Rice (Ph.D., Stanford University, 1982) is Associate Professor in the School of Communication, Information and Library Studies, Rutgers University. He is coeditor or coauthor of *Public Communication Campaigns* (Sage, 1981, 1989), *The New Media: Communication, Research, and Technology* (Sage, 1984), *Managing Organizational Innovation* (Columbia University Press, 1987), and *Research Methods and New Media* (Free Press, 1988). He has published widely in the areas of diffusion of innovations, network analysis, and organizational computer-mediated communication systems.

Dr. Rice was involved in the evaluation of the oral rehydration therapy (ORT) communication health campaigns in Honduras.

*   *   *

What are the most common reasons mass media campaigns do not achieve their hoped-for results, and what are the most common reasons some campaigns are relatively successful?

One reason campaigns fail is that the criteria for success are not clearly defined. Evaluation experts Tom Cook and Brian Flay say that there are three models for deciding what success is: the *advertising model* for primarily determining exposure to the message, the *monitoring model* to determine the intended behavioral effects, and the *experimental model* to determine whether the relationships among the theoretically predicted influences, messages, peer support, and so on are in fact causally linked to attitude and behavior change. There can be no simple answers because there might be success from the advertising model viewpoint but failure from the experimental model viewpoint. For mass media campaigns, the advertising model is usually used, so it is possible to show that there was exposure but perhaps no behavior change.

Targeting of a campaign audience is not usually done in a sophisticated manner. Also, there may not be adequate understanding of the most appropriate media to reach the target audience, and this further limits the chances for success.

The larger environment surrounding youth is not conducive to behavior change. Messages spread, but if the life situation of the young audience is not changed, prosocial messages from the campaign are *tiny* compared to the other countermessages being generated by the environment.

Smokey the Bear created awareness about the dangers of forest fires in the United States, but there are still vast numbers of forest fires and in that sense this campaign failed. Campaigns may create symbols that get disassociated from their original purpose over time. For example, younger people born after the media campaign know about Smokey, but they do not know what he is supposed to mean.

Multitreatment approaches are effective, as shown by the work of the Stanford Heart Disease Prevention Program (SHDPP). Mass media should be used along with community support, bus posters, demonstrations in stores, etc. This kind of campaign requires a major effort by a dedicated group of people, however.

How could present health communication campaign models be improved to make them useful for planning, implementing, and evaluating mass media campaigns?

Several models of public communication campaigns are available, but from a practitioner's point of view a program usually does not follow any single "model." Each campaign follows different theories of persuasion and knowledge transfer based upon the campaign's goals. The SHDPP had a model that was basically a combination of the health belief model and the social learning model.

Most models for campaigns do not make much distinction between long-term and short-term changes. The models are oriented toward short-term strategies and are not process oriented. The SHDPP and the ORT campaigns were implemented in multiple waves, and have shown that the process of change is very complex.

What roles can formative or summative evaluation play in the relative success of a health communication campaign?

Formative evaluation is critical to campaign success. It is vastly underused, and should be a major up-front component of any campaign. With the help of formative evaluation the message can be tailored, the appropriate channels discovered, and the messages and channels directed to the audience at risk and not at the general population.

Formative evaluation is problematic to implement because it is difficult to conduct, and it is difficult to publish such evaluations. Campaign officials want to get going quickly with the campaign's implementation, even though they know that the use of formative evaluation will contribute to greater campaign success in the long run. Formative evaluation also sometimes goes against the values of the message producers, who are convinced of their ability to produce messages even in the absence of information about the target audience.

What are the unique characteristics and special difficulties of preventive health communication campaigns, especially those aimed at high-risk youth?

Health prevention is conceptual, whereas treatment is more tangible. For example, preventing a forest fire is more abstract than fighting forest fires. Prevention is invisible, and so it is particularly difficult. With youth, prevention is especially difficult because they are at a stage in life when they are not trained in health values, their future is heavily discounted, and an unhealthy outcome in later years is totally irrelevant to them. Youth have tremendous peer support for, and against, most kinds of behavior. Some campaigns focus on the reduction of this social influence, by providing skills for fending off social pressures without alienating the group. The problems that youth have are associated with things they have positive feelings about, like emotional and physical stimulation, sex, and risk taking. It is difficult for them to separate the positive aspects and the negative aspects of their behavior.

How do age groupings, fear appeals, audience segmentation, and use of opinion leaders contribute to the design of mass media campaigns targeted to high-risk youth?

Fear appeals can be useful if the fear is transformed to something positive for youth. We must find out what young people like and want, and then show how those positively perceived matters are threatened by undesirable behavior—under these conditions, fear is related to something highly positive.

Audience segmentation is powerful, but the problem is exactly how to define segmentation. Demographic segmentation is not always so useful. New methods of life-style segmentation may be more helpful, and this is the latest trend in audience analysis.

Communication channels have to be specific, like "MTV," not just "TV." Print generally is not very useful in reaching youth.

What is the most successful mass media campaign to change health behavior you have known, and why do you think it worked?

The Stanford Heart Disease Prevention Program is one of the more successful campaigns. The campaign showed persistent behavior changes through its extensive evaluation, as well as treatment changes in target groups compared with control groups. An important reason for success was that the campaign was long term.

What role should federal, state, or local governments play in media campaigns?

The government can do many things to help bring about behavior change, such as regulating the *content* of the media. For instance, cigarette advertising is banned in Finland as it is in the United States. The major contributions of the government are to provide funding and to change (legal) structures in the social environment of the campaign. However, mass media audiences are not so concerned about issues of societal health, and government personnel need to keep this fact in mind when deciding about new legislation.

What organizations and organizational factors contribute to the success or failure of media campaigns?

Historically, the role of *organizations* in the United States is crucial to getting things done on media campaigns. Getting local media activated and involved in a health campaign is important, and it is the individual media organization, such as a local television station, from which we can learn so much. The Ad Council is sometimes criticized for not producing effective campaign messages because they have to contribute unpaid effort, so problems also exist with volunteer effort. Advocacy groups are effective in securing portrayals of health issues in the mass media, but they want these issues to be portrayed only from their points of view, which often are not realistic.

What methods would you suggest for financing media campaigns for health?

The entertainment-education strategy for health campaigns provides one means of financing such campaigns. The entertainment product helps fund the education campaign.

A crucial theme in all media campaigns is the *tension* between the projected collective benefit versus the individual benefit. Even though the ultimate aim of campaigns may be benefits at the individual level, campaigns also project the collective benefits to society. The goal of all media campaigns should be to make the individuals in the target audiences better individuals, not just to find what makes media campaigns work better.

EVERETT M. ROGERS
University of Southern California

ABOUT THE INTERVIEWEE

Everett M. Rogers is Walter H. Annenberg Professor, Annenberg School for Communication, at the University of Southern California. After earning his Ph.D. degree at Iowa State University in 1957, he taught at Ohio State University, the National University of Colombia (Bogotá), Michigan State University, the University of Michigan, and Stanford University, until his move to USC in 1985. He is a specialist in research and teaching on the diffusion of innovations, and he published a book on this topic in 1962 titled *Diffusion of Innovations* (Free Press), which was revised in 1971 and 1983.

Early in his career, Rogers investigated the diffusion of agricultural innovations among farmers in Iowa and in Ohio, and then, since 1963, in Colombia, Brazil, Nigeria, and India. In the 1980s, he studied the adoption and impacts of a new videotext service, the Green Thumb Box, among Kentucky farmers. Currently, he is synthesizing research on the applications of microcomputers in Third World agricultural development.

In recent years, Rogers's interests have also grown to include the role of technology transfer in high-technology industry. One report of his research on this topic is *Silicon Valley Fever*, coauthored with Judith K. Larsen (Basic Books, 1984). He is currently involved in conducting research on the role of the mass media in reporting disasters.

Dr. Rogers has extensive experience with campaigns in the United States and in Third World countries dealing with energy conservation, family planning, and health. He was Coinvestigator of the Stanford Heart Disease Prevention Program for five years in the early 1980s. He has not been involved in campaigns targeted particularly to high-risk youth.

*   *   *

What are the most common reasons mass media campaigns do not achieve their hoped-for results, and what are the most common reasons some campaigns are relatively successful?

Usually campaigns do not achieve success because of unrealistic goals. Goals of 40% or 50% changes in human behavior are impossible. More reasonable objectives might be 3-5% change in a reasonable time frame of several years. We must set feasible objectives to ensure that the hoped-for results of a campaign are achieved. Often we rely on only one channel and one message. Instead, we must use multichannel multimedia messages.

Campaign planners and implementers know a lot about media, but they are often naive about choosing strategies based on the behavioral sciences. They may rely on simple messages. An integrated team is required. Experts are needed on content, on how to make messages, and on behavior change.

For a campaign to be successful, multichannel multimessages are needed in an integrated set of activities, so that they are timed to occur in a planned sequence, over a period of time. Human behavior is rarely changed in a short time period or without repeated exposure to campaign messages.

How could present health communication campaign models be improved to make them useful for planning, implementing, and evaluating mass media campaigns?

No basic paradigm shift is required in communication campaign models, which have been improving over the years. But we need to update these models. For instance, the application of systems theory would be beneficial to integrate various communication campaign models. Systems theory gives a means to integrate the different parts of a campaign. An example is Dr. Ronnie Adhikarya's rat control campaign in Bangladesh in the early 1980s.

What are the unique characteristics and special difficulties of preventive health communication campaigns, especially those aimed at high-risk youth?

Youth think that they are immortal. Youth audiences do not think of death or ill health. They have an inaccurately perceived risk of certain threatening events. Drugs are habituating and, combined with the dispositions of youth, it is very difficult to stop youth from using drugs.

How do factors such as age groupings, fear appeals, audience segmentation, and use of opinion leaders contribute to the design of mass media campaigns targeted to high-risk youth?

Urban young people start using alcohol, cigarettes, and other drugs when they are in middle school, that is, in the seventh or eighth grade (11-12-13 years old). Dr. Andy Johnson's Institute at the University of Southern California aims its smoking prevention campaigns at this age group.

Fear appeals must be utilized with caution. Sometimes only the fear is remembered, and not the constructive message content about how to resolve the fear. For AIDS and drug abuse, fear appeals cannot be avoided. Fear appeals get attention, but they often are not effective in changing attitudes or behavior. We should distinguish between high and low fear appeals, and use them after pretesting messages in formative evaluation.

Audience segmentation is very important. Each segment may be quite different from others, but within a segment the population is relatively homogeneous. For example, campaign segments can be composed of youth, parents, teachers, and police officers who arrest the drug abusers. Age can be used to segment subaudiences of different age groups (11-12-13 years). Such age segments are interested in different matters, they use different media, and their gender and social maturity is different.

An opinion leader strategy can be utilized by a youth audience. Youths do indeed *have* opinion leaders, but these leaders do not have any special qualities that make them easy to reach in designing a media campaign. Teachers can sometimes identify youth opinion leaders, and pilot studies might be conducted to find the characteristics of the leaders.

Incentives/disincentives are complicated to use, but can be useful. We should do more research on the effects of incentives. We could provide incentives through the school system, through the community, and perhaps through the family. Careful study would tell us which combinations actually work.

The bottom line is *interpersonal communication.* Mass media can provide information, but for behavioral change interpersonal communication is usually required. The mass media are a suitable medium that must be used, like rock music, rap music, and so forth. The media mix for youth campaigns should have a high component of music.

What is the most successful mass media campaign to change health behavior you have known, and why do you think it worked?

The SHDPP has been among the most successful communication campaigns. Why? It was financially well endowed, intensive, and multi-phased over a long time period; it used formative evaluation, utilized the mass media efficiently to initiate interpersonal communication, was very daring and original in its concepts and implementation, and was run by a prestigious organization; and skilled people from different disciplines were integrated in a team effort. Unfortunately, all these conditions are seldom found in other media campaigns.

What role should federal, state, or local governments play in media campaigns?

Private agencies in the United States have the money and the expertise, but many long-term campaigns are government sponsored, as government has the clout, committed finances, and other resources. For example, the extensive campaign for AIDS prevention (requiring a large financial commitment) that has been going on in past years could be conducted only by the U.S. government.

What organizations and organizational factors contribute to the success or failure of media campaigns?

Campaign communication is different from other communication activities. Campaigns represent a mobilization of resources in a specific amount of time. Many organizations are not oriented to this focused effort.

Some organizations have credibility problems in a particular campaign. For example, in the case of the interrelation of drug abuse and AIDS, the U.S. government lacks credibility with drug addicts. It seems unlikely that these individuals will now perceive the federal government as their "helpful friend."

The advantages of grass-roots organizations in conducting campaigns are that they are local, they have credibility with the audience, they know local conditions, they can reach the appropriate subsegment of the target audience, they are accustomed to conducting campaigns, and, most important, they are in a position to take risks, such as incurring criticism from a city mayor or the press. A government agency might play it safe, and not take such risks. So there are advantages for a government agency to provide money to a private organization for implementing a media campaign.

For example, an AIDS prevention campaign with drug users may be funded by a city government to a local private organization, which then urges individuals to use clean needles. The federal or city government could not officially recognize that needles exist for drug use, and for the local government to provide clean needles might be perceived as encouraging drug abuse.

What methods would you suggest for financing media campaigns for health?

The ideal of a public communication campaign is a *win-win* situation, where the goals are attained and at the same time the costs of running the campaign are returned. The entertainment-education strategy can often both make money and educate an audience, without the two being in conflict.

Sometimes a product associated with a campaign is sold for a certain price. For example, the SHDPP sold booklets about heart-healthy foods, the Children's Television Workshop sells Muppet dolls, and so on. The problem with considered monetary profit as part of a public communication strategy is that it might interfere with the audience's perception of the credibility of the organization and its campaign.

CHARLES SALMON
University of Wisconsin—Madison

ABOUT THE INTERVIEWEE

Charles Salmon (Ph.D., University of Minnesota, 1985) is an Associate Professor in the School of Journalism and Mass Communication at the University of Wisconsin—Madison. He has worked in evaluation research for the Minnesota Heart Health Program, and served as a research adviser to the National Institutes of Health. During the 1990-1991 academic year, he was a Communication Research Specialist with the Centers for Disease Control's National AIDS Information and Education Program, and a Visiting Professor in Communication Studies at the University of Iowa.

Dr. Salmon has published research articles in such journals as *International Journal of Public Opinion Research, American Behavioral Scientist, Public Opinion Quarterly, Progress in Communication Sciences, Evaluation & the Health Professions, Journal of the Market Research Society, Communication Research, Journal of Advertising Research,* and *Journalism Quarterly,* as well as in the *Communication Yearbook.* He has edited two volumes of research essays, *Information Campaigns: Balancing Social Values and Social Change* and, with Ted Glasser, *Public Opinion and the Communication of Consent* (in press), and is guest editor of a forthcoming issue of *Argumentation,* the journal of the European Center for the Study of Argumentation. Salmon has served as Head of the Communication Theory and Methodology Division and as a member of the Standing Committee on Research for the Association for Education in Journalism and Mass Communication.

Dr. Salmon has worked as an evaluation researcher with the Minnesota Heart Health Program, which focused in part on adolescents, although not specifically on high-risk youth. Recently, he conducted research on the effectiveness of Centers for Disease Control campaigns for AIDS prevention. He is the author of an important textbook on communication campaigns.

* * *

What are the most common reasons mass media campaigns do not achieve their hoped-for results, and what are the most common reasons some campaigns are relatively successful?

A common problem with many campaigns is that they are thought of as being "mass media only" campaigns, which is problematic in two respects. Thinking vertically, such a conceptualization results in an extensive reliance on mass communication to the exclusion of other levels of communication, such as organizational and interpersonal. Effective campaigns have tended to supplement mass communication with a variety of other forms, particularly interpersonal. Thinking horizontally, the second problem with the "mass media only" conceptualization is that it results in an excessive reliance on communication to the exclusion of other forms of social change, such as strategies involving the application of power, engineering, or financial support. Effective campaigns are those that have supplemented communication with alternative strategies perhaps better suited for different audience segments and different types of social problems.

Effective campaigns also must (1) make an issue or problem personally and temporally salient to each individual member of an audience segment and (2) monopolize the information environment, as much as possible, through the use of mutually reinforcing strategies, messages, and channels. Antidrug campaigns are more likely than most to achieve this near monopoly because the issue itself has been elevated to "war" status, thus meriting unusually strong government support and inter-institutional cooperation.

How could present health communication campaign models be improved to make them useful for planning, implementing, and evaluating mass media campaigns?

Although several theoretical models of campaigns exist, few are consistently helpful. For example, the hierarchy-of-effects model is fine in the abstract, but in practice, things do not work in such a linear fashion. Much of the research on persuasion has been conducted in laboratory settings, which do not accurately simulate the real-life environments in which campaigns are actually conducted. Although psychological models are useful in guiding *message* strategies, sociological models, such as diffusion or the knowledge gap hypothesis, may be more useful in guiding overall *campaign* strategies.

What roles can formative or summative evaluation play in the relative success of a health communication campaign?

Exhaustive formative research and clearly articulated goals and objectives greatly increase the probability of a campaign's obtaining results, shown in summative research on campaign impact, that will be viewed as evidence of success. But what is success? When assessing the impact of a campaign, it is important to acknowledge the evaluator's expectations, as there really is no absolute standard about what constitutes a "successful" campaign. Relatively modest changes in knowledge, attitudes, or behavior have been and can be considered indicators of either success or failure, depending upon the expectations of the campaign planners and evaluators. Social marketers targeting high-risk groups should be particularly sensitive to this point. Such campaigners sink considerable time and money into efforts to change the very persons who are the most difficult and resistant to change (for example, persons addicted to nicotine or cocaine).

Commercial marketers, on the other hand, usually allocate resources to target groups that have the *greatest potential for change* in the desired direction. Clearly, the two sets of marketers ought to approach outcome evaluation with entirely different sets of expectations and criteria for success. And they do. But the paradox is that commercial marketers, who are attempting to achieve modest degrees of change with generally receptive target markets, actually appear to have *lower* expectations for success than do social marketers, who often are laboring to achieve massive changes in life-style with generally unreceptive target markets.

What are the unique characteristics and special difficulties of preventive health communication campaigns, especially those aimed at high-risk youth?

What generalizations can we make about successful approaches in campaigns? It is difficult to say. To answer this question in anything but the most general of terms is to deny the importance of an ongoing program of research for each discrete campaign effort. Barriers to effective communication are radically different for different issues and populations, thus limiting the generalizability of findings from one situation to another.

Further, society is dynamic, meaning that today's understanding of attitudes, behaviors, and norms pertaining to even a single issue may be obsolete tomorrow. We can always cite some general principles that have, over the years, become virtual clichés: "Use credible spokespersons," "employ moderate levels of fear appeals," and "segment the audience." But we must consider the merits of each of these principles on an ad hoc basis in the context of the specific issues and populations with which we are dealing.

How do factors such as age groupings, fear appeals, audience segmentation, and use of opinion leaders contribute to the design of mass media campaigns targeted to high-risk youth?

Adolescents have very different reference groups from those of adults, and yet we see campaigns like the Just Say No antidrug effort in which Nancy Reagan acts as a spokesperson. It is difficult to believe that adolescents who are taking drugs will stop merely because Nancy Reagan has told them to do so. She is an important, powerful, and hence credible symbolic figure to the adult power groups running the campaign and perhaps even to some adolescents; however, she may not be a meaningful or credible source in the specific adolescent subculture being targeted for change. Only through specific formative research can the general principle of source credibility be applied in a meaningful manner.

Second, although many studies have employed and advocated the use of fear appeals, we in the social sciences lack the precision to measure— in absolute terms—amounts or doses of fear. The general finding that "moderate" levels of fear seem to be effective is not necessarily generalizable, as "high," "moderate," and "low" levels of fear have not been held constant across studies. Message testing of PSAs is continually needed to determine the threshold of fear beyond which a specific message becomes dysfunctional.

Third, it is inconceivable to run a campaign without relying on some segmentation principle. But segmentation must be appropriate to the specific situation at hand. Too often, we segment in terms of those comfortable and convenient variables, i.e., demographics. This implicitly leads us to speak of "adolescents" as a homogeneous group because certain individuals share the common demographic characteristic of age. As a result, we ask, "How can we reach adolescents?" or "What will work with adolescents?" thereby overlooking the heterogeneity— in terms of psychographics and social class—of this group. Instead, we need to segment in terms of multiple variables (e.g., issue involvement, capacity for change, susceptibility to social pressure, literacy, or level of knowledge) to appreciate fully the power of targeting communications. And it is only through extensive formative research that we can even identify the appropriate variables for segmentation in a particular situation.

What is the most successful mass media campaign to change health behavior you have known, and why do you think it worked?

Many campaigns, such as the Stanford Heart Disease Prevention Program and the Minnesota Heart Health Program, have been commonly defined as successful. And many more campaigns, conducted by industry and involving proprietary data, have been defined so as well. Yet, even if we take advantage of what has worked in the past with other issues and populations, there is no guarantee that communication itself is potent enough to solve every social problem, especially something like drug use.

Earlier in the twentieth century, we learned that communication and enforcement strategies were not sufficient to eradicate alcohol use. Why do we now expect the same strategies to halve the use of other types of drugs? If our efforts do not succeed, we would do well to ponder a sobering question: Do communication campaigns really "fail" or do policymakers fail by deploying communication when it may not have a realistic chance of inducing the type and magnitude of change being sought?

LARRY STEWART
Entertainment Industries Council

ABOUT THE INTERVIEWEE

Larry Stewart is a writer-producer-director who has been involved in campaigns aimed at the entertainment industry to motivate the industry to deglamorize the use of alcohol and other drugs in its television productions. He is a member of the Caucus for Producers, Writers and Directors, which several years ago developed an important white paper on alcoholism, later widely disseminated in the entertainment industry.

Mr. Stewart also coauthored a white paper titled "Let's Have None for the Road," on the issue of drunk driving. He has been an adviser on seat belt use campaigns, and has assisted in the production of PSAs on that topic. He is an officer and member of the board of directors of the nonprofit Entertainment Industries Council.

*   *   *

What are the most common reasons mass media campaigns do not achieve their hoped-for results, and what are the most common reasons some campaigns are relatively successful?

Campaigns are successful when they are well planned, the audience characteristics are studied, and the message is presented in the semantics of the target audience. The key is to know who you are speaking to, and then to speak to them in their language. For campaigns aimed at the entertainment industry, to achieve success one must not spell out exactly how a particular aim is to be accomplished. The how should be left to the creativity and the intelligence of media industry professionals.

Semantics are very important in any campaign. For example, the change in the terminology from "alcohol and drugs" to "alcohol and other drugs" places the issue of chemical dependency in a correct light. For example, there is a clear distinction between the phrases *recovering alcoholic* and *recovered alcoholic.* A "recovered alcoholic" is more positively appreciated by people interacting with such a person. Campaign officials must be aware of the changes taking place in the terminology used, or their credibility will be reduced.

Health professionals should be utilized in devising health behavior campaigns. Professionals are needed to come up with the correct approach and direction, and the correct terminology. It is better to correct a mistake beforehand than to show it to millions of viewers. The involvement of professionals is also helpful in the success of a campaign, because then the campaign tends not to get attacked by other concerned people who may be able to find flaws in the concept, approach, or terminology of a campaign.

How do factors such as age groupings, fear appeals, audience segmentation, and use of opinion leaders contribute to the design of mass media campaigns targeted to high-risk youth?

In the alcohol and drug abuse field, it is important to know the audience demographically. We know at what age kids start using drugs, and how their peer dynamics work. Prevention should start in elementary school, interventions should begin in junior high school, and treatment—if required—should begin immediately at the onset of the need. In the seat belt awareness campaigns, PSAs were made for the nation at large, but a number of videos were made for junior high schools, where vehicle driving usually starts.

Denial is a common difficulty with a target audience in alcohol and other drug abuse. Denial is also evident in the AIDS issue, where it is combined with a high degree of fear. In youth, denial is very common. Fear does not "sell" behavior change, and fear-based messages do not work. For example, the "Frying Egg" PSA has been laughed at by kids who see it. They felt that they were being put down and that they could not take the PSA seriously. Youth have a feeling of invulnerability. Fear tactics do not scare them. Youth are vain and are very concerned about their physical appearance and looking good. We should appeal to that in health campaigns.

Opinion leaders usually have their minds made up on issues and are focused on their activities. It would be more effective to choose an opinion leader who already shares the point of view being propagated.

From the viewpoint of cost-effectiveness and reaching the largest audience, radio is probably the most effective campaign channel. It costs less than TV, and reaches a larger audience. Television is very expensive, and the times that a PSA is aired are very important. It is of little use if a PSA is aired at four in the morning. Radio does not have this kind of prime-time problem. Alternative channels of communication, such as posters, may not be as cost-effective as television shows or movies.

Television and radio should work in conjunction with each other. Interpersonal communication is very important in media campaigns. You cannot just throw a mass media campaign at the audience; someone has to follow up and lobby for it. Star personalities are usually used for community groups where money is to be raised. For other occasions, people who can talk expertly about the issue under consideration are used.

What is the most successful mass media campaign to change health behavior you have known, and why do you think it worked?

Several antismoking campaigns of recent years were very successful. They worked because the people, especially users (smokers), were generally concerned about their health problems, and there was a general trend toward health fitness consciousness. Also, the credibility of the people making pronouncements of statistics and the like, such as U.S. Surgeon General Koop, was helpful. Koop connected the problem to other problems facing society, and was able to scare people, although primarily he was appealing to adults.

The Just Say No campaign was ineffective thanks to its message content, but it was enormously successful in terms of reach. The reason was that Nancy Reagan was involved, and the message was so simple that it absolved parents of responsibility. It was the kid's role to prevent drug abuse, as opposed to the family's.

What methods would you suggest for financing media campaigns for health?

All nonprofit agencies are looking for money from the federal government. Negotiating and fund-raising skills help get this money, and it is this practical type of skill development that would doubtless help the most.

LAWRENCE WALLACK
University of California at Berkeley

ABOUT THE INTERVIEWEE

Lawrence Wallack is Associate Professor in the School of Public Health, University of California, Berkeley. He has published extensively on policy issues related to health promotion and disease prevention. He has worked on developing environmental approaches to the prevention of alcohol-related problems since the mid-1970s. His current primary research interest is the role of mass communication in addressing public health problems, particularly the use of alcohol, tobacco, and other drugs.

Dr. Wallack was an adviser to former Surgeon General C. Everett Koop on the development of recommendations to address drunk driving. He has been a consultant to the World Health Organization, various foundations, and many local, state, and federal agencies.

Dr. Wallack is the recipient of several awards, including the Beryl Roberts Prize in Health Education (1980); Peer Recognition Award, Society of Public Health Educators, Northern California (1983); and Early Career Award, Community Health Education Section, American Public Health Association (1984). He has appeared on *Nightline, Oprah, Today, Good Morning America, Cable Network News,* and numerous local news and public affairs programs to discuss his research and to comment on social policy issues regarding alcohol, tobacco, and other drugs.

* * *

What are the most common reasons mass media campaigns do not achieve their hoped-for results, and what are the most common reasons some campaigns are relatively successful?

People tend to look at mass media as a quick and easy solution to social and health problems. Unfortunately, these problems are complex, being rooted in a cultural, political, and economic context, and require a range of strategies, including changes in public policy. Mass media are an important tool when used in addition to, rather than instead of, community organization, coalition building, and advocacy to develop or change public policy.

Mass media are definitely an important tool for addressing alcohol and drug problems, particularly among youth. But we need to be thoughtful and creative in how we choose to use this resource. First, we know that media play an important role in agenda-setting. The media have the ability to focus attention on an issue, get people thinking and talking about the issue, and stimulate support for action. Second, we know generally that mass media when used alone are not very effective at changing behaviors, especially when those behaviors are complex or tightly held. Third, we know that media have a tendency to reduce health and social issues to problems of life-style or personal behavior and to minimize the policy or environmental aspects. Fourth, the history of public health interventions suggests that policy- and community-level approaches tend to have the greatest potential for creating change.

How could present health communication campaign models be improved to make them useful for planning, implementing, and evaluating mass media campaigns?

Academics have models, but the people who actually manage campaigns do not utilize these models for the most part. The keys to the success of mass media campaigns are good program planning principles, audience analysis, needs assessment, and the whole range of formative evaluation and consumer inputs.

In putting all these things together, several possibilities emerge. First, broad social marketing campaigns that are tailored to get a specific message to a specific audience in a specific way play an important role. These campaigns can get people's attention and focus them on the issue. Basic principles of social marketing, such as formative research, audience analysis, and market segmentation, must be used to create a message that resonates with the intended audience.

Second, mass media must be used as an advocacy tool to stimulate policy-level changes. "Media advocacy" techniques attempt to reframe problems such as teenage alcohol use away from being seen as behavioral problems to being seen as social policy issues. The ultimate intent is to focus attention on the behavior of the "drug pusher" rather than the user, whether the pusher is selling cocaine, alcohol, or tobacco.

For example, the introduction of Powermaster, a high-alcohol-content malt liquor, in the African-American community resulted in this community reframing the alcohol issue as one of corporate greed and exploitation. Media coverage did not focus on teens using this "high-octane" beverage, but on the behavior of Heilman, the company that produced the product. Media attention resulted in the product's being withdrawn and the federal regulatory agency's reconsidering its rules on how these products may be advertised.

In the area of drugs, several groups are trying to develop media strategies that raise the issue of how minority groups are portrayed on news and public affairs programs. The larger issue here is why some groups are disproportionately shown as drug pushers and drug users. The key education that is seen as being necessary is not only on the evils of drugs but on the larger social issue of racism.

The key issue is how best to use the mass media to stimulate change in the broader social and political context in which health behavior takes place. This means trying to alter not the behavior of individuals with problems but the behavior of those whose decisions largely determine the information environment in which individuals make health decisions. This means turning the media spotlight on the "manufacturers of illness" so that the contradictions of public policy (e.g., advertising of beer to youth) can become a focal point of attention. The innovative strategy of media advocacy that focuses on the responsibility of the system needs to become a primary strategy, and social marketing campaigns, though important and necessary, should have a lower priority in claiming resources.

What are the unique characteristics of preventive health communication campaigns, especially those aimed at high-risk youth?

Health campaigns typically try to "unsell" a behavior. We try to tell people *not* to do something. It is a fundamentally different kind of problem from when advertisers try to induce someone to *do* something—to buy a product. The primary risk factors for mortality and morbidity in our society have to do with social conditions. Health status is closely linked to social and economic concerns. These are complicated issues, and campaigns will not succeed unless they address them.

How do factors such as age groupings, fear appeals, audience segmentation, and use of opinion leaders contribute to the design of mass media campaigns targeted to high-risk youth?

In early childhood, kids might decide not to use alcohol or other drugs, but in early adolescence this viewpoint may change. Mass media messages are weak in reinforcing an initial attitude. What are we doing to enhance the quality of life for our youth by providing them with quality education, safe homes, and family life? Media can be used to reinforce the idea that drug use is not a good idea, but other interventions are needed along with media messages to address these larger issues.

There is some advantage to fear appeals, especially moderate fear appeals. The key to effective fear appeals is that they should not develop a high level of anxiety. A quick, accessible outlet also should be provided for the resolution of the anxiety or to reduce fear. The AIDS issue is a good example. To get the population to attend to the AIDS epidemic, fears appeals were required, but safe sex and other responses were emphasized as coping responses, with some success.

However, long-term appeals to youth usually do not succeed. Changing behavior now to improve health status 10 years or more from now simply does not appeal to youth! We must create incentives for adopting a new behavior that relate to the immediate environment of youth, such as peer groups, families, and, in some cases, opinion leaders.

Mass media are useful for directing people toward more in-depth kinds of interpersonal resources. Mass media may be effective for recruiting people to sign up for a treatment program or encouraging them to call an 800 number.

The primary functions of mass media are agenda-setting and awareness creation. Billboards can be an important resource that has been overlooked. Direct mail also is sometimes an appropriate way of reaching people. It is cheap and can be easily targeted to specific segments. Formative research has to be done in an open-ended way to find out what channels are used by the target audience; the media campaign can then be designed around these findings.

What is the most successful mass media campaign to change health behavior you have known, and why do you think it worked?

The Healthy Babies Campaign in Washington, D.C., which tried to reduce infant mortality, was relatively successful. Jerry Wishnow conducted this campaign. He created an "incentives book" that was heavily advertised through newspapers and television. Teenagers were provided with redeemable coupons to buy goods for their babies at discounts. They had to get the coupons validated by a physician or a health care provider in order to show evidence of prenatal visits. The short-term effect of the campaign was a decrease in infant mortality rates. The campaign was apparently successful in part because it used a lot of local community channels, was localized, and used creative incentives.

What role should federal, state, or local governments play in media campaigns?

The federal government should continue to create and support national campaigns that get out a positive message and that contribute to the agenda-setting function for an issue. The federal government also can exercise a leadership role in promoting the wider use of approaches such as social marketing.

What organizations and organizational factors contribute to the success or failure of media campaigns?

Much of the work of the Ad Council and other large organizations has not been effective. If a problem is defined as an individual-level problem, then the mass media are increasingly thought of as a solution. This may be counterproductive to the ultimate redress of the problem. The media should help us *redefine* a problem, set the agenda on the nature of this health problem in our society, and start people thinking about the structural and the corporate reasons underlying the problem (these seldom get addressed). As long as industry and government remain involved, it may be possible to achieve progress on the issue. The mass media have to identify the problem as a shared responsibility, and show in their messages that all the blame does not lie with the individual.

What methods would you suggest for financing media campaigns for health?

The tobacco, alcohol, and other industries, such as the automobile industry, should keep aside a percentage of their gross profits, and out of that a fund should be created for the development of public education, including material for media messages. This funding is justified because all advertising gets a tax break, so in effect advertising is at a discount rate and the U.S. government is subsidizing it. The public should get value out of these tax breaks.

PART FOUR

Implications and Future Directions

Our comparative study of campaigns and the experts who shape them has resulted in a confirmation of some basic principles for health communication campaign success that seem to be fairly common across topical areas, and also has identified a number of issues that need further exploration. In this final section, we present some implications for future campaign design and for research.

Implications for Campaign Design

It is hoped that the generalizations listed in Part II can be applied to campaign design and execution. For instance, it may be helpful to create a "checklist" of desirable campaign features based upon these generalizations. Then any campaign design can be compared against this checklist while it is still in its earliest stages.

Reference could also be made in campaign planning sessions to the text of these generalizations in their entirety. They are meant to provoke questions as much as to answer them, so no clarifying discussion has been added in Part II. However, campaign designers might well want to

167

review selected interview transcripts or literature citations in this report for more background and inspiration about the 27 generalizations.

Such a checklist might be especially useful as a *strategic planning device* for a campaign developer or advisory committee. Economics, special campaign circumstances, or the philosophies/values of those conducting or sponsoring a particular campaign might preclude addressing certain generalizations, but the evidence compiled in this study suggests that there is a "critical mass" for campaign effectiveness that can be moved forward by the use of such a strategic planning process, and by including attention to as many of the 27 generalizations as possible.

There also appears to have been an infusion recently of entertainment principles and technologies into the design and execution of campaigns, and a number of the 27 generalizations represent approaches with which filmmakers or commercial advertisers would be quite comfortable. Also, several of our 29 interviewees have primary identification with the entertainment industry, and indeed are comfortable moving within the workings of this highly specialized industry when involved with health campaigns.

It is likely that such entertainment approaches will become even more common in the near future for mass media health campaigns. A strategy that has come to be known as *entertainment-education* represents a formalization of this crossover, and will be discussed further at this point.

THE ENTERTAINMENT-EDUCATION APPROACH

In the last 15 years, an entertainment-education strategy has been developed by a group of campaign designers in the United States and abroad, and this approach has been used in various nations to spread ideas about topics such as family planning, female equality, adult literacy, and other subjects. This strategy began with a television soap opera in Peru in 1969, *Simplemente María (Simply Mary)* and was carried forward by Miguel Sabido, a Mexican television producer-director-scriptwriter. He created six different year-long soap operas that were broadcast throughout Latin America from 1976 to 1983. They each achieved high audience ratings and seemed to have important audience effects.

In 1984-1985, the educational soap opera strategy spread to India with the broadcast of *Hum Log (We People)*, a very popular television soap opera about family planning. Several other nations have since used this strategy in television or radio soap operas to present health information to large audiences.

Patrick Coleman and his colleagues at the Johns Hopkins University School of Public Health applied the entertainment-education strategy to popular music, first in Mexico and Latin America with "Cuando Estemos Juntos" ("When We Are Together") by Tatiana and Johnny, then in the Philippines ("I Still Believe" by Lea Salonga), and then in West Africa, with a popular song, "Choices," about adult sexual responsibility. An evaluation study in Mexico showed that the Tatiana and Johnny song was played an average of 15 times a day over a period of several months, and this massive, repeated exposure led to knowledge, attitude, and overt behavior effects concerning sexual abstinence and contraception among the target audience of Mexican teenagers.

The basic strategy seems to be quite adaptable, and has been utilized in comic books, music, and various broadcasting genres. For example, the Harvard Alcohol Project promoted the idea of the "designated driver" on U.S. prime-time television in 1989-1990 by getting this concept incorporated in episodes of some 35 prime-time television series. An evaluation research study showed a resulting increased use of the designated driver idea by the U.S. public (Winston, 1990). Note that the Harvard Alcohol Project did not produce its own television series to communicate the designated driver idea, but rather requested voluntary incorporation of the story idea. This approach has been increasingly used by the so-called "Hollywood lobbyists" documented by Montgomery (1988). For instance, in 1990 the Entertainment Industries Council conducted a number of briefings with groups of writers in the television industry, both at the TV networks and at large Hollywood TV production companies, to discuss issues of AIDS and drug abuse. Current research and local service programs were presented in brief, layperson-oriented form, and several story ideas actually found their way to the air as a result.

The entertainment-education strategy thus can be utilized by influencing scriptwriters, directors, and producers of a television series to incorporate one's health education concept into their programs. As Montgomery's (1988) book chronicles, a growing number of "Hollywood lobbyists" seek to persuade U.S. television programs to give attention to their causes: alcoholism, AIDS prevention, mental health, the environment, gay and lesbian rights, and teenage contraception. These entertainment-education activities have not been evaluated as to their effects on the target audience, however, with the exception of the Harvard Alcohol Project. The Entertainment Industries Council and the Human Interaction Research Institute currently are involved in a joint venture on a project that is *identifying* a wide range of news and entertainment media health communication strategies, and then *documenting* their use.

Notice that the designated driver campaign was promoted by a prestigious institution, the Harvard University School of Public Health. The credibility of the source/sponsor does make a difference in health communication activities, as is also illustrated by the cases of the North Karelia Project, the Stanford Heart Disease Prevention Project, and the Johns Hopkins University's Population Communication Services project in entertainment-education music for teenagers.

Further reasons for the success of the Harvard Alcohol Project as Hollywood lobbyist (that is, in convincing the scriptwriters, producers, and directors to incorporate the designated driver concept into a primetime television show) are that (a) the Hollywood entertainment media community has itself suffered from alcohol-related problems, so the problem of alcoholism has some visibility already, and (b) Mothers Against Drunk Drivers (MADD) has been extremely successful in influencing the U.S. media to stress the problem of drunk driving. Also, the Harvard Alcohol Project attacked drunk driving but not alcohol consumption, and thus did not threaten the alcohol advertising incomes on which the media are dependent.

A COMPARATIVE SYNTHESIS OF MENTAL ILLNESS MEDIA CAMPAIGNS

There are many topical areas in which the results of our research might be utilized. Some of these topics move beyond changing the health behavior of the direct target audience per se into the even more complicated arena of changing knowledge, attitudes, and behaviors about some third-party groups in society, so that their physical or psychological health needs can be better met. One good example of this involves increasing understanding and reducing stigma of severe mental illnesses, such as schizophrenia and manic-depressive illness.

Most Americans depend on television as their primary source of information about subjects such as mental illness (Backer, 1984, 1986). This fact has led to great interest among professionals and consumers about the role that the mass media can play in enhancing the quality of life for severely mentally ill people. Providing accurate information and sympathetic portraits of the mentally ill can reduce stigma, help to increase employment and social interaction opportunities for mentally ill people, and increase willingness of the public to support the investment of public resources in providing appropriate treatment (Backer, 1984).

Since 1985, one of the authors (Thomas Backer) has collaborated with the Former First Lady Rosalynn Carter and the Carter Center in Atlanta on explorations of the positive role that the mass media can play in mental health. At the First Rosalynn Carter Mental Health Policy Symposium, strategies were identified for media and mental health professionals to use (Backer, 1986). In 1988, the fourth symposium focused on strategies for developing community partnerships with the mass media, using a comparative synthesis approach. Ideas for mental health campaigns were derived from presentations on successful campaigns about drug abuse, AIDS, seat belt awareness, Alzheimer's disease, and family values on television (Backer, 1988a).

More recently, the comparative synthesis research presented in this book was used to identify specific strategies that might be tried to enhance media campaigns concerning mental illness. A number of these campaigns have been mounted in recent years, including long-term efforts of the National Institute of Mental Health, the National Mental Health Association, and the American Mental Health Fund. Following are some sample strategies not yet tried in past or current campaigns:

- Radio PSAs with network, station, and celebrity involvement have been little used in mental illness campaigns. Good examples of success can be seen in the Entertainment Industry Council's AIDS and IV Drug Abuse Campaign for the National Institute on Drug Abuse.
- A Hollywood-based, consumer-run office to work collaboratively with the media, as has been used successfully by the National Council on Families and Television and by many other groups, has not been tried. As mentioned, those involved in such activities are often called "Hollywood lobbyists" (Montgomery, 1988).
- Tie-ins with existing print and audiovisual media disseminated through the public schools have been little tried for mental health topics.
- The use of a special film as a fund-raising tool (with sponsored "premieres" and special showings) has not been tried, as was done with *There Were Times, Dear* (a film about Alzheimer's disease that has raised more than $2 million through public event screenings in recent years).

- There have been few efforts to distribute guidelines for writers and other media professionals concerning mental illness through relevant professional organizations and unions.

These strategies were explored further in the October 1989 Rosalynn Carter Symposium. At the meeting, the emphasis was on media depiction of the mental health problems of the elderly (Backer, 1989). Several of the strategies identified in the previous year's comparative synthesis, such as preparing guidelines for writers, were developed for implementation. For instance, written guidelines for depiction of mental health professionals, service institutions, and families of the mentally ill were distributed by the Carter Center to more than 2,500 Hollywood film and television professionals. Thus over a five-year period a considerable effort has been made to identify what needs to be done in mass media presentations about mental illnesses and to begin implementing potentially useful strategies taken from other health campaigns. A follow-up conference, set in Hollywood and designed to bring together mental health and mass media experts, was held in summer 1990. The National Alliance for the Mentally Ill also developed a multipart media campaign that incorporates the above strategies (Backer, 1988b), including distribution of written guidelines to the print press.

Implications for Future Research

The 27 generalizations in Part II are not presented as unchanging realities about what works and what does not in health communication campaigns with mass media components. Even though cross-validated in a number of campaigns, these strategies are still only partially understood. For instance, as detailed further below, the role of organizations in campaign effectiveness has not been much studied. Also, generalizations about campaigns have not been analyzed as to their relative importance across different campaign topics, or for the "cumulative effect" they might have. Many empirical issues of this sort remain unsettled.

Other topics for future research include the following:

- Word-of-mouth and promotional messages that are pro-use, including advertising of legal (for adults) drugs such as alcohol and tobacco, are also part of the environment in which media campaigns operate. How can campaigns be designed to intercept and neutralize such messages (e.g., addressing street myths about drug effects and exploring the potential of counter-advertising or media advocacy opportunities)? How can the array of pro-use messages for a particular topic and target audience be taken into account in planning a mass media campaign?

- What additional strategies might be formulated? Press conferences, product placements in films and television shows, and public relations strategies such as mentions of campaigns on television and radio news shows or in print media are among the possibilities. Some fairly specific options for intervention already are available. For example, what might be the effect of encouraging set designers and production designers in films or TV shows to use prevention-oriented posters on their sets, so that they will appear on the screen? Such an effort could be facilitated by a union or other media-based organization.

- How do community involvement and interpersonal strategies interweave with other mass media health campaign features? How does the mix of campaign strategies need to vary depending upon other components of the overall message system?

- How can strategic planning among several organizations contribute to large-scale systems change in various health behavior areas—including as components of mass media campaigns, community involvement, interpersonal strategies, policy/legislative changes, and other factors that all interweave to change structures, values, and behaviors?

- How can mechanisms be developed for the pretesting and evaluation of mass media campaigns, including those that take advantage of the comparative synthesis approach used here? The federal government at one point sponsored a Health Messages Testing Service. Could such a program be productively restarted?

- What additional evaluations of the long-term impacts of media campaigns should be undertaken? What might we learn from revisiting children exposed to the Just Say No campaign as young adults, for example?

- For fast-changing health issues such as AIDS, how do media campaigns respond to changing science and medical practice?

IMPACT OF ORGANIZATIONS ON
HEALTH COMMUNICATION CAMPAIGNS

One topic that has been little studied, but that emerged as important in our comparative synthesis research, is that of the critical roles and activities of organizations in developing, implementing, and evaluating health communication campaigns. Television networks, public health agencies, universities, media professional or trade societies, and advocacy organizations (often including those specific to mass media and health) are among the organizations that influence the success or failure of a campaign.

Backer and Rogers (in press) report on a study, also funded by the Office for Substance Abuse Prevention, conducted to investigate the impact of organizations on mass media health behavior campaigns, by bringing together campaign experts with leading experts on organizational behavior and management sciences. To begin this process, a workshop was held on April 10, 1990, in Washington, D.C. Six highly successful mass media health campaigns in health-related areas were explored at this workshop, detailing their histories, successes, and challenges, and how various organizations were involved with them. Organizational theory then was used to analyze the campaigns, searching for common strategies and principles.

From this workshop, six case studies of organizational impact on mass media campaigns emerged, with six commentaries by the participating management experts. These six case studies and commentaries form the main content of Backer and Rogers (in press):

1. Campaign: Media Advertising Partnership for a Drug-Free America

Case study author: Thomas E. Backer, Human Interaction Research Institute, Los Angeles

Commentator: Robert Golembiewski, Department of Political Science, University of Georgia, Athens, Georgia

2. Campaign: Project STAR

Case study authors: Mary Ann Pentz and Thomas Valente, Institute for Health Promotion and Disease Prevention, University of Southern California, Los Angeles

Commentator: Leonard Goodstein, Goodstein Consulting, Washington, D.C.

3. Campaign: Family Planning and Health Program in Turkey

Case study author: Lawrence Kincaid, Center for Communication Programs, Johns Hopkins University, Baltimore

Commentator: David Krakhardt, Johnson School of Business, Cornell University, Ithaca, New York

4. Campaign: Stanford Heart Disease Prevention Project

Case study author: June Flora, Department of Communication, Stanford University, Stanford, California

Commentator: Peter Vaill, Department of Management Science, George Washington University, Washington, D.C.

5. Campaign: Drug Abuse Resistance Education (DARE)

Case study author: Everett M. Rogers, Annenberg School for Communication, University of Southern California, Los Angeles

Commentator: Mark Kiefaber, Burke Associates, Greensboro, North Carolina

6. Campaign: Harvard Alcohol Project

Case study author: Kathryn Montgomery, Woodrow Wilson International Center for Scholars, Washington, D.C.

Commentator: Jean Bartunek, Department of Organizational Studies, Boston College, Chestnut Hill, Massachusetts

LOOKING AT CAMPAIGN DESIGNERS/EXPERTS

Further exploration also is possible regarding factors that pertain to our 29 campaign designers/experts. A more detailed examination of their common philosophies, backgrounds, and operating styles would be desirable, along with explorations of differences that pertain to different topical areas or bases of operation. A sociometric analysis of how these professionals interact with one another might be very fruitful, since they often work together in various combinations. Understanding of the "politics" and "sociology" of mass media campaigns depends importantly on further inquiry into these factors.

Characteristics of mass media health campaign designers/experts that seem especially fruitful for further research include the following:

- *Commitment:* The campaign designer/expert's determination to make the campaign happen despite limited resources, resistance, or even limited interest in the campaign itself or the subject it addresses can be of importance. Campaign designers/experts frequently develop specializations in particular campaign areas because of highly personal commitments to improving health or preventing health problems in particular areas. When other resources are limited, the energy of "passionate commitment" can in itself be enough to keep a campaign going.
- *Deeply held values:* The values of the campaign designers, as well as their prior experiences with campaigns and their interaction with other campaign designers, may also be worthy of study. Our interviewees took theory seriously—though this often meant they strongly rejected a theory or

theories in general. Their professional points of view strongly influenced the campaigns they designed.

- *Charisma:* Most campaign designers/experts, even if not proficient public speakers or personally charismatic individuals, somehow project a high degree of energy about their work, and this creates a certain potential for visibility and persuasiveness that helps to sell the campaign, and often serves as a substitute for financial resources.

- *Concentrated viewpoint:* Most of the campaign designers/experts we interviewed have strongly held sets of values and beliefs about both the content and the process of the campaigns they are working on. This can be an advantage in helping them to motivate others who work alongside them, but it can also be a disadvantage if it blinds them to helpful criticism or danger points.

Specific analysis of our 29 experts on these and other factors may help to increase our understanding of the complex dynamics by which individuals can have a critical impact on campaign initiation and success.

Some of the campaigns we have discussed are to some extent "one-person shows." Although many people may be involved in designing and executing them, there is often one principal figure whose charisma, concentrated viewpoint, and commitment drives the entire project. What differences might there be between these one-person shows and more broadly integrated team efforts?

The factors listed above are all often commented upon informally, and they clearly have a high degree of impact. But they have *not* been studied in systematic research, or included in theories about campaign design and effectiveness.

The type of study reported here, our subsequent study on organizational factors, and some of the research designs we have alluded to here do not constitute conventional empirical research. This is qualitative research that may help set the frame for empirical research to come. In the meantime, these are factors that, if better understood, can provide better means for analyzing and understanding mass media health campaigns of the past and present, and for planning campaigns of the future.

References

Atkin, C., & Arkin, E. (Eds.). (1988). *Proceedings of the Mass Communications and Health: Conflicts and Complexities Conference.* Rancho Mirage, CA: Annenberg Center.

Atkin, C., & Wallack, L. (1990). *Mass communication and public health: Complexities and conflicts.* Newbury Park, CA: Sage.

Backer, T. E. (1984). *Proceedings: Portraying mentally ill people in films and television shows.* Rockville, MD: National Institute of Mental Health.

Backer, T. E. (1986). Powers untapped: Mass media depiction of mental illness. In J. Houpt (Ed.), *Proceedings of the First Rosalynn Carter Mental Health Policy Symposium.* Atlanta: Carter Center.

Backer, T. E. (1988a). *Community partnerships with the media: What works and what doesn't.* In J. Houpt (Ed.), *Proceedings of the Fourth Rosalynn Carter Mental Health Policy Symposium.* Atlanta: Carter Center.

Backer, T. E. (1988b). *Working with the media: A manual for AMI affiliates.* Arlington, VA: National Alliance for the Mentally Ill.

Backer, T. E. (1989, November). *Mass media and the elderly: Depicting mental health issues on entertainment television.* Paper presented at the Fifth Annual Rosalynn Carter Symposium on Mental Health Policy, Atlanta.

Backer, T. E. (1991). Knowledge utilization: The third wave. *Knowledge: Creation, Diffusion, Utilization, 12,* 225-240.

Backer, T. E., & Rogers, E. M. (1992). *Organizational aspects of media health campaigns.* Manuscript submitted for publication.

Backer, T. E., Rogers, E., & Sopory, P. (1990). *Impact of organizations on mass media health behavior campaigns* (final report). Los Angeles: Human Interaction Research Institute.

Backer, T. E., Rogers, E., & Sopory, P. (1991). *Mass media health campaigns and their designers: Annotated bibliography.* Los Angeles: Human Interaction Research Institute.

Bandura, A. (1986). *Social foundations of thought and action.* Englewood Cliffs, NJ: Prentice-Hall.

Beniger, J. R. (1983). *Trafficking in drug users: Professional exchange networks in the control of deviance.* New York: Cambridge University Press.

DeJong, W., & Winston, J. A. (1989). *Recommendations for future mass media campaigns to prevent preteen and adolescent substance abuse.* Unpublished paper, Harvard School of Public Health, Center for Health Communication.

Downs, A. (1972). Up and down with ecology: The "issue-attention cycle." *Public Interest, 28,* 23-50.

Farquhar, J., Maccoby, N., Wood, P., & Alexander, J. (1977). Reducing the risk of cardiovascular disease. *Journal of Community Health, 3,* 100-114.

Flay, B. R. (1986, May). *Mass media and smoking cessation.* Paper presented at the Annual Conference of the International Communication Association, Chicago.

Gantz, W., Fitzmaurice, M., & Yoo, E. (1990). Seat belt campaigns and buckling up: Do the media make a difference? *Health Communication, 2,* 1-12.

Hyman, H., & Sheatsley, P. (1947). Some reasons why information campaigns fail. *Public Opinion Quarterly, 11,* 412-423.

Kerr, P. (1986, November 17). Anatomy of the drug issue: How, after years, it erupted. *The New York Times,* p. A1.

Lefebvre, C., & Flora, J. (1988). Social marketing and public health intervention. *Health Education Quarterly, 15,* 229-315.

Maccoby, N., Farquhar, J., & Solomon, D. (1984). Community application for behavioral medicine. In E. Gentry (Ed.), *Handbook of behavioral medicine.* New York: Guilford.

Maccoby, N., & Solomon, D. S. (1981). Heart disease prevention: Community studies. In R. E. Rice & W. J. Paisley (Eds.), *Public communication campaigns.* Beverly Hills, CA: Sage.

Mendelsohn, H. (1973). Some reasons why information campaigns can succeed. *Public Opinion Quarterly, 37,* 50-61.

Merriam, J. E. (1989). National media coverage of drug issues, 1983-1987. In P. J. Shoemaker (Ed.), *Communication campaigns about drugs: Government, media and the public.* Hillsdale, NJ: Lawrence Erlbaum.

Montgomery, K. (1988). *Target prime-time.* New York: Oxford University Press.

Nadelmann, E. A. (1989, September 1). Drug prohibition in the United States: Costs, consequences, and alternatives. *Science,* 939-947.

Neuman, W. R. (1990). The threshold of public attention. *Public Opinion Quarterly, 54,* 159-176.

Office for Substance Abuse Prevention. (1989). *Prevention plus II.* Rockville, MD: Author.

Puska, P., Koskela, K., McAlister, A., Mayranen, H., Somolander, A., Moisio, S., Viri, L., Korpelainen, V., & Rogers, E. M. (1986). Use of lay opinion leaders to promote the diffusion of health innovations in a community programme: Lessons learned from the North Karelia Project. *Bulletin of the World Health Organization, 64*, 437-446.

Puska, P., McAlister, A., Koskela, K., Pallonen, U., Vartiainen, E., & Homan, K. (1979). Mass media and smoking cessation. *International Journal of Health Education, 22*, 2-10.

Puska, P., McAlister, A., Pekkola, J., & Koskela, K. (1981). Television in health promotion: Evaluation of a national programme in Finland. *International Journal of Health Education, 24*(4), 2-14.

Puska, P., Nissinen, A., Salonen, J., Tuomilehto, J., Koskela, K., McAlister, A., Kottke, T., Maccoby, N., & Farquhar, J. (1985). The community-based strategy to prevent coronary heart disease: Conclusions from the ten-year North Karelia Project. *Atherosclerosis Reviews, 21*, 109-117.

Reinarman, C. (1988). The social construction of an alcohol problem: The case of Mothers Against Drunk Drivers and social control in the 1990s. *Theory and Society, 17*, 91-120.

Reinarman, C., & Levine, H. G. (1989). The crack attack: Politics and media in America's latest drug scare. In J. Best (Ed.), *Images of issues: Typifying contemporary social problems* (pp. 115-137). New York: Aldine de Bruyter.

Rice, R. E., & Atkin, C. K. (1989). *Public communication campaigns* (2nd ed.). Newbury Park, CA: Sage.

Rogers, E. M. (1983). *Diffusion of innovations* (3rd ed.). New York: Free Press.

Rogers, E. M., & Chang, S. (1991). Media coverage of technology issues. In L. Wilkins & P. Patterson (Eds.), *Science as symbol and media images in a technology age.* Westport, CT: Greenwood.

Rogers, E. M., & Dearing, J. W. (1988). Agenda-setting research: Where has it been, where is it going? In J. A. Anderson (Ed.), *Communication yearbook 11* (pp. 555-594). Newbury Park, CA: Sage.

Rogers, E. M., Dearing, J. W., & Chang, S. (1991). The agenda-setting process for the issue of AIDS. *Journalism Monographs.*

Rogers, E. M., & Storey, J. D. (1987). Communication campaigns. In C. Berger & S. Chaffee (Eds.), *Handbook of communication science.* Newbury Park, CA: Sage.

Salmon, C. (1990). *Public information campaigns.* Newbury Park, CA: Sage.

Shoemaker, P. J. (Ed.). (1989). *Communication campaigns about drugs: Government, media and the public.* Hillsdale, NJ: Lawrence Erlbaum.

Shoemaker, P. J., Wanta, W., & Leggett, D. (1989). Drug coverage and public opinion, 1972-1986. In P. J. Shoemaker (Ed.), *Communication campaigns about drugs: Government, media and the public.* Hillsdale, NJ: Lawrence Erlbaum.

Signorielli, N. (1988). *Health and the media: Images and impact.* Paper presented at the Mass Communications and Health: Complexities and Conflicts Conference, Annenberg Center, Rancho Mirage, CA.

U.S. Department of Health, Education and Welfare. (1979). *Healthy people: The surgeon general's report on health promotion and disease prevention.* Washington, DC: Government Printing Office.

Weisman, A. P. (1986, October 6). I was a drug-hype junkie. *New Republic*, 14-17.

Winston, J. A. (1990). *The designated driver campaign developed nationally by the Harvard Alcohol Project.* Cambridge, MA: Harvard University, School of Public Health.

About the Authors

Thomas E. Backer is President of the Human Interaction Research Institute, a nonprofit organization devoted to studies of knowledge utilization, planned change, and health communication. He is also Associate Clinical Professor of Medical Psychology, UCLA School of Medicine.

Everett M. Rogers is Walter H. Annenberg Professor, Annenberg School for Communication, University of Southern California, and a member of the board of directors of the Human Interaction Research Institute.

Pradeep Sopory received his master's degree in communications management from the Annenberg School at USC, and is currently a doctoral candidate in the Department of Communication Arts, University of Wisconsin—Madison.

The authors have extensive experience in scholarly research and field interventions concerning the design and effects of health communication campaigns, both in the United States and abroad. Backer and Rogers are currently completing a project, supported by the Office for Substance Abuse Prevention, that investigates the role of organizational factors in the conduct of health communication campaigns.